Dylan Evans is a writer and well-known atheist. He
received his PhD in Philosophy from the London
School of Economics in 2000. He has taught at various
universities around the world, written several popular
science books, and set up two companies. He has
been a teacher, a Lacanian psychoanalyst and a
novelist. He is a distinguished supporter of the British
Humanist Association.

His other books include: *Introducing Evolutionary
Psychology* (with Oscar Zarate) (1999); *Emotion: The
Science of Sentiment* (2001); *Placebo: The Belief Effect*
(2003; republished as *Placebo: Mind over Matter in
Modern Medicine* (2004); *Risk Intelligence: How to live with
uncertainty* (2012) and *The Utopia Experiment* (2015).

ATHEISM
ALL THAT MATTERS

ATHEISM

Dylan Evans

Also available in ebook

Contents

Preface

I am a natural-born atheist. As a child, I believed in Father Christmas for a while, but never in gods. When I first learned, at the age of six, that humans are 60 per cent water, this prosaic fact didn't dismay me at all but sent a thrill down my spine. Likewise, when I discovered shortly after that our thoughts are nothing but patterns of electro-chemical activity swirling round in our brains, I delighted at the sheer materiality of it all. I confess that I also took especial pleasure in tormenting my poor granny with these facts, which she found hard to reconcile with her simple Catholic faith and her belief in human specialness.

Like many children, I found church extremely boring, and on those rare occasions when I was forced to go (by my school), I found the stories about Jesus and his disciples bizarre and nonsensical. When I was teenager, I became interested in Zen Buddhism, and part of what attracted me about it was that it didn't require me to believe in gods.

But then, at the age of 17, I had an intense conversion experience. I was sitting at my desk in my bedroom one evening, trying to do my homework, when all of a sudden I felt my body bathed in waves of cosmic love, and I felt forgiven. Tears came to my eyes, and for the first time in my life I thought to myself: 'There is a god!'

I had just been expelled from school, and now my friends' parents wouldn't let them see me for fear I would be a bad influence on them. After years of being a model pupil I was now officially a bad boy, and it is clear to me now that what I experienced that evening in my bedroom was simply the result of a powerful wish for forgiveness. But at the time it felt utterly compelling.

Other things played a part, too, in preparing my brain for that mystical experience. Very cleverly, my granny had taken advantage of my interest in Zen Buddhism to send me a book about a Catholic priest who had spent a year in a Zen monastery in Japan. As I read it, I wondered if perhaps all religions led to the same goal and I became less scornful of Christianity. Soon after, I converted to Catholicism. That was my granny's revenge for all those moments when I had tormented her as a child.

I went off to university to do a degree in religious studies. But it soon became clear that was not enough to satisfy my growing fervour, and after a year I dropped out and went off to Ireland to train to be a priest. It was a very strict missionary order with the fierce-sounding name of the Legionaries of Christ, but I loved the military discipline and the austere spirituality. After a few months, we went through a week of spiritual exercises. Based on a sequence of meditations and prayers devised by St Ignatius of Loyola in the 16th century, these exercises are designed to lead you to a point of intense personal conviction and commitment.

For a week, there was complete silence, meaning not only that the novices weren't allowed to talk to each other, but also that we couldn't even look each other in the eye. There were five one-hour meditations every day in addition to mass, benediction and other rituals.

Everything was designed to lead up to the final meditation on the last day of the retreat, when we would practise 'seeing god in nature'. When that moment finally came, it was a glorious spring evening and we were allowed to do our meditation while walking round the grounds of the seminary.

It was warm and the sun was setting in a clear blue sky. The birds were singing and the scent of the spring blossoms wafted through the air. If ever there was a moment when I was going to see god in nature, this was it.

And you know what I saw? A beautiful sunset. That was it. And it was enough. It was more than enough; it was perfect. And it suddenly occurred to me that to foist the idea of a god onto this perfection would be to ruin it, to force a superabundant nature into a shabby little human concept, like cramming a bunch of wild roses into a shoddy little wooden box.

I knew immediately that my spiritual director wouldn't like this. So I didn't tell him at first, and tried to continue as I had before. But it was pointless. Something had changed in me. I had lost my faith as irrationally as I had gained it, in a strange but compelling personal experience.

When I did eventually tell my spiritual director what had happened to me that spring evening, he realized there was no point in me staying. He put me on a flight back to England the very next day. And after my few years holidaying in the land of religion, I went back to being the atheist I always was.

It's amazing what the brain can do.

A note on style

In this book I will not follow the widespread practice of talking about 'belief in God'. Instead, I will usually speak of 'belief in gods'. There are two important differences here. First, I see no reason to capitalize the word *god*. Secondly, I prefer to speak of *gods* in the plural, rather than *god* in the singular. To understand why, consider unicorns. If you wanted to find out whether someone believed that such creatures exist, you would probably ask: 'Do you believe in unicorns?' You would certainly *not* ask 'Do you believe in unicorn?', let alone 'Do you believe in Unicorn?' Even if you believed that there was only one unicorn in the whole universe, you would still probably say 'I believe in unicorns'. You might add 'I believe that there is only one unicorn in the universe', just to be clear, but you certainly wouldn't say 'I believe in unicorn'. Even if the unicorn had a name – let's say his name was Charlie – you wouldn't say 'I believe in Charlie'. By analogy, it is just plain odd for anyone to say, 'I believe in God'.

1

Who cares?

Isn't that [an agnostic] just an atheist without balls?

Stephen Colbert[1]

Most 'isms' involve a belief in something. Dualism is the belief that bodies and minds are made of different kinds of stuff. Communism is a *set* of beliefs, including the conviction that we are inexorably heading towards a moneyless, classless and stateless society. Atheism is unusual in that it involves *dis* belief. An atheist is someone who doesn't believe there are any gods.

Why do we need a word to indicate the *lack* of a belief in gods? After all, we don't have a word to indicate the lack of belief in a stateless society; nobody describes himself or herself as an 'acommunist'. This question has puzzled some people, including some famous atheists. Jonathan Miller, a writer and theatre director, once remarked that he never felt the need define himself as a 'non-believer', since his atheism 'was not at any point a rejection of anything'.

> *'I'm rather reluctant to call myself an atheist. And it's not because I'm embarrassed or ashamed of it, or because I fear for my life as I might have done in the olden days if I had announced that I was. Nor have I any reason to think that I might be socially disabled in a way that I once might have been. No – the reason that I'm so reluctant is that atheism itself has acquired almost sectarian connotations, and it hardly – as far as I can see – seems worthwhile having a name for something that scarcely enters my thoughts at all. For myself, as for many people, it's only in the light of such current controversies with regard to belief that I've found myself willing to explicitly articulate my disbelief.'* [2]

The same thought has been voiced by the astrophysicist and science communicator Neil deGrasse Tyson. 'It's odd that the word *atheist* even exists,' he says in a popular YouTube video. 'I don't play golf. Is there a word for non-golf players? Do non-golf players gather and strategize? Do non-skiers have a word and come together and talk about the fact that they don't ski? I don't; I can't do that. I can't gather round and talk about how much everybody in the room doesn't believe in god. I just don't, I don't have the energy for that.'[3]

Likewise, the philosopher Daniel Dennett says: 'I don't like the term atheist because it usually means somebody who is going around upbraiding people and trying to force people to listen to his arguments as to why there is no god. I don't think there is a god, so I am an atheist, but I don't make a deal of it. It's not that I passionately believe there isn't a god, it's that, of course there isn't a god, but so what?'[4]

What Miller, Tyson and Dennett seem to have in mind here is a particular *kind* of atheist. Tyson imagines a bunch of atheists sitting round and discussing their unbelief. Dennett pictures an argumentative atheist who is constantly picking fights with believers. There are certainly atheists who behave like this, but to tar all atheists with the same brush is silly. Some atheists are happy to keep their beliefs to themselves, and do not feel the need to huddle around with other atheists for comfort.

Despite what Miller, Tyson and Dennett say, there is in fact a very good reason why we need the word *atheist*, but don't need words for people who aren't communists or don't play golf. Of all the people who have ever lived, only a tiny minority have been communists or played golf, so there is no need for a word to denote the vast majority that have not. When it comes to religion, however, things are very different. Almost everyone who has ever lived has believed in the existence of a god or gods. In every society we have ever known, atheists have been a tiny minority – and they continue to be a minority today. According to the *CIA World Factbook*, atheists made up only 2 per cent of the world population in 2010, although 'non-religious' people accounted for a further 9.7 per cent.

Like other minorities, atheists have often been ridiculed, persecuted, imprisoned and even murdered for daring to be different. Unlike Jonathan Miller or Neil deGrasse Tyson, most atheists throughout history have been forced to confront and label their disbelief, and have often paid a high price for doing so. They have not enjoyed what Miller calls the 'luxury of thoughtless disbelief'.

Coming out as an atheist

'I am an atheist, out and out. It took me a long time to say it. I've been an atheist for years and years, but somehow I felt it was intellectually unrespectable to say one was an atheist, because it assumed knowledge that one didn't have. Somehow, it was better to say one was a humanist or an agnostic. I finally decided that I'm a creature of emotion as well as of reason. Emotionally, I am an atheist. I don't have the evidence to prove that God doesn't exist, but I so strongly suspect he doesn't that I don't want to waste my time.'

Isaac Asimov, interview in *Free Inquiry*, spring 1982.

So it is disingenuous – even myopic – to claim, as Miller and Tyson do, that we don't need a word to designate people who don't believe in gods. Even today, few atheists have the luxury of growing up in a relatively tolerant society. And to call yourself an atheist need not imply that you are part of a movement and like to 'gather and strategize' with other atheists, as Tyson wrongly implies. An atheist is simply someone who doesn't believe there are any gods. This is a sociologically, historically and philosophically important position, and we need a word for it, no matter what a few privileged and out of touch intellectuals may say.

▶ How many atheists are there?

According to the best current estimates, atheists make up around 2 per cent of the world population. When we look at this on a country-by-country basis, however, we find that the percentage of atheists varies widely in different parts of the world. The picture in Europe is very mixed, for example. A Eurostat Eurobarometer poll in 2010 asked people to choose between three options:

A 'I believe there is a god.'

B 'I believe there is some sort of spirit or life-force.'

C 'I don't believe there is any sort of spirit, god or life-force.'

The table below shows the percentage of people in each group for some European countries. As you can see, levels of religious belief vary widely.

	A	B	C
France	27	27	40
Germany	44	25	27
Ireland	70	20	7
Italy	74	20	6
Spain	59	20	19
Sweden	18	45	34
United Kingdom	37	33	25

Europe, however, is somewhat of an exception. It is the most secular of all continents, and levels of religious belief are much higher everywhere else. Africa is the most devout continent, and Ghana the most religious country in the world, with 96 per cent of the population claiming to be religious. The number of people who identify as atheist is so small that the number doesn't even register; officially, it is 0 per cent. Nigeria is not far behind, with 93 per cent of the population professing a religious belief, and only 1 per cent of the population identifying themselves as atheist. Nevertheless, there are a few African countries with significant numbers of atheists, such as South Africa and Botswana.

Latin America is also a very god-fearing continent, with 83 per cent of Mexicans and 65 per cent of Brazilians saying they were Catholic in 2010. But faith is fading; in 1970 the figures were 96 per cent and 92 per cent respectively. In Central America the church's decline is even more marked: its share has slipped below half in Honduras and is not far behind in El Salvador and Nicaragua. But the main reason for the decline of the Catholic church in these countries is not a rise in the number of atheists but the rise of other Christian 'brands', especially miracle-working Pentecostalism.

The success of these Protestant brands is due in large part to clever marketing: Central America's feel-good evangelical mega-churches have growing television audiences as well as packed weekly congregations.

The Middle East is also full of believers. It is still very rare in the Arab world for anyone to describe themself openly as an atheist, as this can lead to ostracism by family and friends, and even draw retaliation from Islamist hard-liners and the authorities. There are a few countries where most people are Muslim and yet atheists can live safely, such as Turkey and Lebanon. But none gives atheists legal protection or recognition. According to sharia law, former Muslim atheists are guilty of apostasy, and eight states, including Iran and Saudi Arabia, have the death penalty on their statute books for such offences. Arguments for the death penalty are usually based on a Hadith, 'The Prophet said: whoever discards his religion, kill him.'

But is not just the developing world where atheists continue to be in a small minority. The United States too is still a bastion of the Christian faith. Despite the many changes that have rippled through American society over the past 70 years, belief in gods has remained high and remarkably stable. Between 1944 and 2011, the proportion of people answering 'yes' to the question 'Do you believe in God?' never fell below 92 per cent. Nevertheless, freedom of religion is a constitutionally guaranteed right in the United States, and the First Amendment states that: 'Congress shall make no law respecting an establishment of religion, or prohibiting the free exercise thereof.' Freedom of religion is also closely associated with separation of church and state, a concept advocated by Thomas Jefferson.

The most atheist country in the world is China, which has been governed by the Chinese Communist Party since 1949. The Communist Party is an atheist organization, which scorns both major world religions and traditional Chinese faiths, and destroyed countless temples and relics during the Cultural Revolution between 1967 and 1977. Nevertheless, five religions are now officially recognized in China: Buddhism, Taoism, Islam, Protestantism and Roman Catholicism. A survey conducted by Shanghai University in 2007 found that 59 per cent of people above the age of 16, or about 600 million people, considered themselves irreligious. A 2012 poll by WIN/Gallup International reported that 47 per cent of Chinese respondents described themselves as 'convinced atheists', although other surveys have put the number of atheists in China at between 8 per cent and 14 per cent. The wide disparity among these estimates underscores the difficulty of accurately surveying the religious views of a nation of over a billion people, but also points to some problems related to identifying religious belief specifically.

▶ Will the real atheists please stand up?

Collecting reliable statistics on the number of atheists in any given country is difficult mainly for the following three reasons:

- people might be unwilling to admit their true beliefs for fear of social disapproval

- people understand terms like *belief* and *atheism* in different ways, so two people may give different answers to the same question, even though their beliefs are in fact identical

- subtle differences in the way that pollsters phrase questions about religious belief can lead to wide discrepancies between poll results.

The first problem affects both strongly religious and strongly atheist countries. As we will see, atheists still face widespread discrimination and even persecution in many parts of the world so they may not always answer surveys about religious beliefs honestly. But fear of social disapproval can work the other way too. In China, for example, where the Communist Party retains a strong hold on many areas of public life, people may be afraid to admit they believe in gods when responding to an official survey.

The second problem applies everywhere, since words like *belief*, *atheism* and *god* are understood in widely different ways. Take the word *belief*, for example. Many people think of belief in binary terms; you either believe something or you don't, and there are no shades of grey in between. I call this 'the all or nothing fallacy'. It is a fallacy because you don't need to be completely certain of something in order to state, honestly, that you believe it. Even the Bible acknowledges this; 'Lord, I believe; help thou mine unbelief!' says the father of a boy possessed by spirits when Jesus tells him that a cure is possible if the father believes it is (Mark 9:24). The existence of some doubt does not make this man an unbeliever. It's all a question of degree. But how much doubt is allowed before the man no longer qualifies as one of the faithful? And how much more doubt can an agnostic entertain before he or she becomes a de facto atheist?

The well-known atheist Richard Dawkins suggests that we think of religious belief as a spectrum of probabilities. At one end of the spectrum is complete certainty that God exists. At the other end is complete certainty that God does not exist. In between there is a continuum, which Dawkins punctuates with several milestones:

▶ Very high probability but short of 100 per cent: de facto theist. 'I cannot know for certain, but I strongly believe in God and live my life on the assumption that he is there.'

▶ Higher than 50 per cent but not very high: technically agnostic but leaning towards theism. 'I am very uncertain, but I am inclined to believe in God.'

▶ Exactly 50 per cent: completely impartial agnostic. 'God's existence and non-existence are exactly equiprobable.'

▶ Lower than 50 per cent but not very low: technically agnostic but leaning towards atheism. 'I do not know whether God exists but I'm inclined to be sceptical.'

▶ Very low probability but short of zero: de facto atheist. 'I cannot know for certain but I think God is very improbable, and I live my life on the assumption that he is not there.'

The key point about Dawkins' spectrum is that the threshold for belief is not total certainty but somewhat less; you can still count yourself as a theist without being 100 per cent convinced that there is a god. Conversely, it is possible to be an atheist and yet admit that there is some small probability that a god may exist. As the Australian philosopher Jack Smart has noted, a failure to acknowledge this may lead a person who is really an atheist to 'describe herself, even passionately, as an agnostic'[5]. Smart's point is that it would be *misleading* for someone who believes that there is no more than a 5 per cent chance that gods exist to describe herself as an agnostic. A person who attributes such a small chance to the existence of gods is, to all intents and purposes, an atheist.

Doubt and certainty

'I think it's much more interesting to live not knowing than to have answers which might be wrong. I have approximate answers and possible beliefs and different degrees of certainty about different things, but I am not absolutely sure of anything and there are many things I don't know anything about, such as whether it means anything to ask why we're here [...] I don't have to know an answer. I don't feel frightened by not knowing things, by being lost in a mysterious universe without having any purpose, which is the way it really is as far as I can tell.'

Richard P. Feynman, 'The Pleasure of Finding Things Out', BBC TV *Horizon* documentary, 1981.

In addition to differences in the way that individual words are understood, statistics on atheism are also affected by differences in the way that questions are phrased. In 2001 the English and Welsh census used the highly leading question 'What is your religion?', which assumes that everyone holds a religious belief of some sort or another. Over 70 per cent of the population responded 'Christian', a far higher percentage than nearly every other significant survey or poll on religious belief in the past decade. When YouGov asked the same question in March 2011, the figure was still high, with 61 per cent of people in England and Wales ticking a religious box. But when the same sample was asked the follow-up question 'Are you religious?', only 29 per cent said 'yes'. That suggests that around half of those whom the census counted as having a religion may well not be religious at all.

It is also worth noting that asking people whether they are religious or not is not quite the same as asking whether they believe in god. Some people may believe in god and yet not describe themselves as religious because they do not go to church very often. There are also atheist religions; in most forms of Buddhism, for example, there are no gods, simply human beings that become enlightened.

These three problems with collecting reliable statistics about atheism suggest that current survey data probably underestimate the true number of atheists in the world. Nevertheless, it is still safe to say that atheists continue to represent a very small minority of the world's population. And this is not likely to change any time soon.

▶ Discrimination

Like other minorities, atheists have often been persecuted for daring to be different. In Europe between the 14th century and 18th century, those accused of atheism or blasphemy could face torture and execution. For example, a Polish nobleman, Kazimierz Łyszczyński, was tried for atheism and executed in 1689 after writing a treatise called 'The non-existence of God'. During the 19th century, atheists in Britain were subject to discrimination; the poet Percy Bysshe Shelley was expelled from the University of Oxford in 1811 after publishing a pamphlet entitled 'The Necessity of Atheism', and subsequently was denied custody of the children of his first marriage because of his atheism.

But persecution of atheists is not simply a thing of the past. And nor is it limited to mere social disapproval. Take the case of the Indonesian civil servant Alexander Aan. Though raised as a Muslim, by the age of 11 he was already clear that he didn't believe in a god. In January 2012, at the age of 29, Aan posted a simple question to an atheist Facebook group he had founded: 'If God exists, why do bad things happen? ... There should only be good things if God is merciful.' He also declared heaven, hell, angels and devils to be 'myths', and said that Muhammad was 'attracted to his daughter-in-law'.

The Indonesian Council of Ulema saw these posts and reported Aan to the police for blasphemy. A few days later, an angry mob attacked him on his way to work, causing police to take him into protective custody. He was charged with 'disseminating information aimed at inciting religious hatred or hostility', 'religious blasphemy' and 'calling for others to embrace atheism'. Aan later issued a public apology for his Facebook posts and converted to Islam, but despite this he was sentenced to two and a half years' imprisonment.

Offending religious feelings

Many countries have laws against blasphemy or 'offending religious feelings'. Why is religion singled out for special protection? After all, there are no similar laws against offending political feelings or aesthetic feelings. In most western countries free speech is regarded as a higher good than protecting religious feelings and the law upholds the right to say things that others may find offensive, including mocking religion. But in other parts of the world this is not the case. The real debate is twofold: is it immoral to mock or satirize religion and, if this is the case, would this constitute a reason to criminalize such behaviour?

The Muslim world doesn't have a monopoly on religious intolerance; atheists suffer from discrimination in the west too. In the United States, six state constitutions include religious tests that would effectively prevent atheists from holding public office, and in some cases being a juror or witness in a trial. Although these have not generally been enforced since the early 19th century, few US politicians have been willing to identify themselves as atheists, and several polls have shown that about 50 per cent of Americans would not vote for a presidential candidate if he were an atheist. A 2006 study at the University of Minnesota showed atheists to be the most distrusted minority among Americans, with 40 per cent of respondents characterizing atheists as a group that 'does not at all agree with my vision of American society'. This was higher than for any other group, including Muslims (26 per cent) and homosexuals (23 per cent). Commenting on these findings, Joe Foley, co-chairman for Campus Atheists and Secular Humanists, remarked that 'atheists are one of the last groups remaining that it's still socially acceptable to hate'.

Discrimination towards atheists seems to be growing in Russia. Following the 1917 Bolshevik Revolution, the USSR became the first state in history to pursue, as a matter of public policy, the elimination of religion and its replacement with universal atheism. The communist regime confiscated religious property, ridiculed religion, harassed believers and propagated atheism in schools. Since the collapse of the Soviet Union in 1991, however, Russia has seen an upsurge of religious belief. Between 1989 and 2013, the proportion of Russians who identify themselves as non-believers fell from over 70 per cent to less than 30 per cent (although this would still put it in the top two or three countries in the world in terms of the proportion of atheists, according to most polls).

Pussy Riot, a Russian feminist punk rock protest group, fell foul of this sea-change in Russian society when three of the members were arrested after staging a performance in Moscow's Cathedral of Christ the Saviour in 2012. They were convicted of 'hooliganism motivated by religious hatred' and sentenced to two

▲ Members of the Russian radical feminist group Pussy Riot try to perform at the Cathedral of Christ the Saviour, Moscow, in 2012, in a protest against the Russian government's policies.

years' imprisonment. Their decision to perform in a cathedral was a protest at the increasingly close connection between organized politics and organized religion. Like many leaders before him, President Putin has consolidated his power by cosying up to the religious authorities. In 2013, he introduced a tough new anti-blasphemy law that allows for fines of up to 300,000 roubles (about £5,000 or US$9,000) and imprisonment for up to three years for public acts that 'are committed with the aim of offence to the religious feelings of believers'. But Putin wouldn't have been able to do this without the resurgence of religious belief in Russia.

In Africa, things are equally bleak. In 2012, a 27-year-old atheist activist who reportedly administered the Egyptian Atheists Facebook page was arrested after a mob gathered outside his home demanding his arrest for insulting religion. Alber Saber was then attacked in prison after a guard told the other prisoners what he had been charged with. He was later convicted of blasphemy and sentenced to three years in prison.

In India in 2012, a renowned sceptic called Sanal Edamaruku was charged with 'hurting the religious sentiments of a particular community' after he debunked a supposed miracle. Thousands of Christians had believed that a crucifix at a church in Mumbai cried real tears, until Edamaruku showed that the dripping water came from a leaky drain. Soon after, Edamaruku moved to Finland to avoid the possibility of an indefinite prison sentence.

Outside western Europe, then, atheists still face discrimination and persecution. It takes real courage to declare oneself an atheist in countries as diverse as Russia, the United States and Indonesia. It is not just a question for idle philosophical debate, but of radical self-expression and personal freedom.

Arguing about gods

The more we refine our understanding of God to make the concept plausible, the more it seems pointless.

Steven Weinberg[6]

So far, I've sidestepped the crucial question of what, exactly, we mean by the word *god*. If atheists are people who don't believe there are any gods, we clearly need to know what these things are that they don't believe in. Unfortunately, there is no simple or widely agreed way of answering that question. Most believers would probably agree, though, that a god is, at the very least, a supernatural agent. In other words, a god is some kind of being who has thoughts and desires, but who is not subject to the normal laws of physics.

This is a pretty minimal definition of the word, but it still rules out some uses of the term. When some New Age folk speak vaguely of god as 'the ultimate', for example, it isn't clear whether they mean a personal god, with thoughts and desires, or just some vague impersonal force or energy. Likewise, scientists and others sometimes use the word *god* to mean something so abstract and unengaged as to be hardly distinguishable from the laws of nature. Einstein once said that he believed in 'Spinoza's god who reveals himself in the orderly harmony of what exists, not in a god who concerns himself with fates and actions of human beings'[7]. But this is to stretch language so much that even an atheist could believe in some kind of god, which makes a nonsense of the whole idea. Of course, anyone is free to use the word *god* in that way if they like, but it makes the concept of god not so much wrong as unimportant. To quote the physicist Steven Weinberg: 'The more we refine our understanding of God to make the concept plausible, the more it seems pointless.'

Is money your god?

Sometimes people use the word *god* to denote anything that someone reveres, as in 'money is your god' or 'celebrities are the gods of today'. Atheists revere different things, according to their value systems, and so they could be said to have gods in this loose sense of the term, but this is just a poetic way of talking. When I say that atheists don't believe in gods, I mean that they don't believe in the kind of supernatural beings with thoughts and desires that religions have typically venerated for thousands of years.

In this book, then, I assume that when people say they believe in gods, they mean at the very least that they believe in supernatural beings with thoughts and desires. This is clearly not the whole story, though. Ghosts, angels and genies also satisfy this definition, but they are not usually thought of as gods, so there must be something else that separates gods from other kinds of supernatural agent. Perhaps gods are supposed to be more powerful than ghosts and angels, or perhaps gods are distinguished from other supernatural agents by their desire to be worshipped (kind of like ghosts with big egos). Different people will have different views on this. It hardly matters for our purposes, however, since atheists don't believe there are any supernatural agents at all, whether of the god type or any other. It would be very odd for an atheist to believe in ghosts, for example.

The problem of defining exactly what people mean when they talk about gods can be illustrated by looking at the wide variety of gods that different cultural traditions have described. Take the Hindu gods, for example. There are a baffling variety of such beings, from Ganesh, who has a human body but the head of an elephant, to Hanuman, a talking monkey. They all have supernatural powers of various kinds, such as the ability to change form at will and cast thunderbolts as weapons. Then are the Aztec gods like Quetzalcoatl, who resembles a feathered serpent, and Tlaloc, with bulging eyes and jaguar fangs. The Greek gods are more humanlike in form, but they are immortal and constantly meddle in human affairs by causing thunderstorms and deflecting arrows. The Norse gods include such imposing figures as Odin, who wields a spear that never misses its target, and Thor, with his mountain-crushing, thunderous hammer. Then there are the Chinese gods, the gods of Ancient Egypt, and the many deities of the Yoruba people in Nigeria. The list goes on and on.

All these mythological systems are polytheistic, which means they assert the existence of many gods. The earliest religions for which we have good archaeological evidence were all polytheistic. The first recorded example of monotheism – the belief that there is only one god – seems to be the cult of Aten promoted by the Egyptian pharoah Amenhotep IV in the 14th century BCE. Amenhotep (subsequently known as Akhenaten) forbade the worship of other gods, which was a radical departure from centuries of Egyptian religious practice. The new religion was short-lived, however; Akhenaten's son Tutankhamun lifted the ban on the cult of other gods soon after he came to power.

It was not until the emergence of Judaism in the seventh century BCE that monotheism became a firmly established form of religious belief. Christianity inherited the belief in one god from Judaism, and Islam from both Christianity and Judaism. These three 'Abrahamic' religions are not the only forms of monotheism still alive today, however. Some forms of Hinduism hold that the many Hindu deities are merely avatars or expressions of one ultimate god, and Sikhism is thoroughly monotheistic. It is the Abrahamic religions, however, and above all Christianity, that have played the greatest part in the history of atheism. With the exception of some ancient Greek philosophers, the most famous atheists in history have lived in, and rebelled against, Christian societies. There were some outspoken atheists in the Muslim world, such as Ibn al-Rawandi (827–911), Al-Razi (854–925) and Al-Ma'arri (973–1058), but few of their writings survive to the modern day.

There is something about the all-encompassing nature of monotheism, and particularly the Abrahamic forms of monotheism, that seems to prompt a clearer expression of atheism in response. Perhaps it is easier, psychologically speaking, to deny the existence of a single god than to deny the existence of many. Richard Dawkins famously quipped that everyone is an atheist about most of the gods that humanity has ever believed in, but 'some of us just go one god further'[8]. This is only true, strictly speaking, for monotheists; a Hindu would have to go a lot more than 'one god further' to become an atheist. But the point is a good one; even a Hindu denies the existence of most of the gods that have been worshipped throughout history. Quetzalcoatl, Tlaloc, Zeus, Apollo, Odin and Thor play no part in his belief system.

When I say that monotheism is 'all-encompassing', I mean that it makes claims to exclusivity that polytheistic systems don't. When Amenhotep declared Aten to be the only true god, he forbade the worship of all other gods. The emergence of Judaism is synonymous with the worship of Yahweh as the only true god. This seems to have occurred in the seventh century BCE, as indicated by the removal of the image of Asherah from the temple in Jerusalem under King Hezekiah (reigned 715–686 BCE). Before then, archaeological evidence and biblical texts suggest there were still some Israelite factions who were comfortable with the worship of Yahweh alongside local deities such as Asherah and Baal. Christians and Muslims have also been zealous about forbidding the worship of any other gods beside their own. Monotheism thus almost always takes the form of what the psychologist Robert Jay Lifton called 'ideological totalism' – 'the conviction that there is just one path to true existence, just one valid mode of being, and that all others are perforce invalid and false'[9].

There are secular kinds of totalism too; Marxism, Leninism, Maoism and Fascism have all been similarly intolerant of other viewpoints. Whether religious or secular, however, totalists 'feel themselves compelled to destroy all possibilities of false existence as a means of furthering the great plan of true existence to which they are committed', wrote Lifton[10]. And when it comes to religious forms of totalism, these other 'possibilities of false existence'[11] include not just belief in other gods, but also belief in no gods at all. In other words, Christians have been just as hostile towards atheists as towards Muslims, Jews and polytheists – often more so. And so have Muslims and Jews.

Personally, it is this totalism that I find most objectionable about monotheism. I don't really care what other people believe; I just object when they try to impose their beliefs on me or on others. I find many polytheists easy to get on with in this respect; they tend to be more accepting of other peoples' beliefs (though not always; witness the militancy of certain Hindu nationalists). Indeed, I often find polytheists more congenial than some of my fellow atheists, who can be just as intolerant of those with different beliefs as the monotheists they condemn. The question of how atheists should approach those with other beliefs is a difficult one, and I will return to it in Chapter 5.

▶ Leaps of faith

Many atheists present their rejection of belief in gods as a supremely rational move. That is, they claim that their atheism is the conclusion of examining the evidence and arguments for and against the existence of gods and concluding, dispassionately, that there are no such things.

There is a corresponding tradition in Christian thought of providing arguments in favour of the opposite conclusion. In this section I will discuss some of these arguments, and the atheist rebuttals, but first I want to consider a prior question that is often neglected by those in who engage in such debates: to what extent does anyone ever *really* base their belief or disbelief in gods on rational considerations?

As a child, I never believed in gods. My childhood atheism was not the result of any process of reasoning, but just something I felt in my bones, a brute belief with no logical justification. Later, when I became a Christian, my conversion was equally irrational, the result of an intense mystical experience that simply overwhelmed any rational thought. And when I lost my faith and reverted to my natural-born atheism, I did so as irrationally as I had gained it, in a strange but compelling personal experience.

I suspect that this is true for many, and perhaps even most atheists. We may like to present our atheism as the sober conclusion of a process of careful reasoning, and such reasoning may well have played some part in leading us to reject the existence of gods, but this is rarely the whole story, or even the main plot. Atheists may, in fact, be just as irrational in arriving at their beliefs as most Christians, Muslims, Jews and Hindus.

Very few people seem to change their beliefs about gods as the result of rational argument. I have attended many debates between atheists and Christians, and never once have I observed anyone standing up at the end of the debate and announcing that, after calmly considering the points put forward by the other side, they have now decided to change their views on the matter. The atheists walk away from such debates even

Arguing about gods

more convinced than before that the whole idea of god is nonsense, and the Christians depart with a deeper and more passionate faith in the existence of a benevolent and all-powerful creator.

Of course, the explanation for this intransigence *could* be that the arguments against the existence of gods are overwhelming, but that Christians are simply much less rational than atheists and so impervious to their arguments. And indeed this seems to be the view of some atheists, who apparently consider themselves paragons of rationality. These atheists get very annoyed if you suggest that atheism is just as much a belief system as Christianity or Hinduism, even though that is, strictly speaking, just what atheism is – a collection of beliefs organized around the contention that there are no such things as gods. What they object to, in such a characterization, is the implication that their beliefs are just as arbitrary and unfounded as the beliefs of Christians and other theists. But every belief system must ultimately be founded on some set of axioms that are simply assumed, and not argued for, on pain of infinite regress. Atheists who deny this are unwilling or unable to expose the assumptions that they take for granted.

Atheists who are more willing to probe their fundamental assumptions may admit that they take as their starting point a basic principle of reasoning known as Occam's razor. This states that, when you are attempting to adjudicate between competing hypotheses, you should choose the simplest one. This often shifts the burden of proof in a discussion. A frequently cited but probably

Are atheists more intelligent than believers?

In 2013 scientists published a review of 63 studies of intelligence and religion[12] and concluded that there was an inverse relation between religiosity – having religious beliefs, or performing religious rituals – and intelligence. In other words, non-believers tend to score higher than religious people on intelligence tests. Why is this? Some scientists suggest that 'religious beliefs are irrational, not anchored in science, not testable and, therefore, unappealing to intelligent people who "know better"'. But another explanation is that those with high IQs have greater self-control and are able to do more for themselves, and so do not need the psychological benefits that religion provides.

apocryphal story about a conversation between the mathematician Pierre-Simon Laplace and Napoleon illustrates how Occam's razor may be applied to the claim that gods exist. According to the story, when Napoleon asked Laplace why, in the course of such a large work on the system of the universe, there was no mention of its creator. Laplace is supposed to have replied: 'I had no need of that hypothesis.' In other words, given the choice between two theories with equal explanatory power – one in which the universe is governed simply by the laws of physics, and one in which there is, in addition to the laws of physics, also a creator god – it is sensible to choose the former theory because it is simpler.

It is interesting to note that William of Ockham himself, from whom Occam's razor takes its name, was a theist.

However, unlike many theologians of his time, Ockham did not believe that the existence of a god could be logically proven on the basis of rational arguments. Unlike science, he argued, theology was a matter of revelation and faith. 'The ways of God,' wrote Ockham, 'are not open to reason, for God has freely chosen to create a world and establish a way of salvation within it apart from any necessary laws that human logic or rationality can uncover.'[13]

Faced with this position, it is pointless to appeal to Occam's razor as the ultimate justification for atheism. And the same kind of problem applies equally to every argument between atheists and theists in the end. It is always open to theists to dispute the ultimate assumptions on which atheists base their arguments, or even to assert that the existence of gods is beyond the realm of rational argument altogether.

Writing in the 19th century, the philosopher Søren Kierkegaard speculated that rational thought would never be enough to motivate religious belief. 'When thinking turns toward itself in order to think about itself, there emerges, as we know, a scepticism,' he noted; but this kind of sceptical thinking just 'runs in circles'[14]. Rational thought could only take one so far; faith could only be attained by leaping beyond these limits. But perhaps the same thing applies to unbelief too; perhaps atheism also requires its own leap of faith.

This is not to say that there are no good arguments on either side. We must be careful to distinguish between the *context of discovery* (the psychological story about how a particular person comes to adopt or reject a given belief) and the *context of justification* (the reasoning process whereby a given hypothesis is confirmed or not). The latter is important, whether or not it plays a decisive role in the former. But while we examine some of the arguments put forward by believers and atheists, it is worth keeping in mind how unlikely these are to change anyone's mind.

▶ Christian arguments

The Christian tradition of constructing arguments for the existence of a single, all-powerful creator god dates back at least as far as St Anselm, a Benedictine monk who became Archbishop of Canterbury in 1093. Anselm proposed what has become known as the *ontological argument*, which goes like this:

1 God is by definition a being greater than any other we can conceive of.

2 If God existed only in the mind, then we could conceive of a greater being; namely, one who also existed in reality.

3 Therefore, God exists.

This is a very strange kind of argument. It attempts to prove the existence of something not on the basis of observation, but on the basis of a mere definition. It seems odd to think that the definition of a concept, however exalted, could guarantee the existence of anything corresponding to that definition. And yet philosophers have struggled to pinpoint the precise point at which the argument breaks down.

The most famous refutation of the ontological argument was put forward a hundred years after Anselm by another Benedictine monk, Gaunilo of Marmoutiers. Guanilo pointed out that the same line of reasoning could be used to prove the existence of, say, the perfect desert island:

1 The perfect desert island is by definition greater than any other desert island we can conceive of.

2 If the perfect desert island existed only in the mind, then we could conceive of a greater desert island; namely, one that also existed in reality.

3 Therefore, the perfect desert island exists.

This is patently absurd, and so, Guanilo concluded, Anselm's argument must be absurd too.

The ontological argument is not cited very often by believers today. Far more influential in Christian thinking is another line of reasoning that goes by the name of the *argument from design*. This is still widely used today in so-called 'creation science'. The argument starts with the observation that living things exhibit the same kind of complex design that we observe in certain human artefacts, such as clocks and watches. Just as watches are designed for telling the time, eyes are designed for seeing and leaves are designed for photosynthesizing. And just as watches are composed of many interlocking parts, each of which plays a part in serving the overall function of telling the time, so eyes are composed of lenses, pupils and photoreceptors, all of which contribute to the overall purpose of seeing.

▲ William Paley (1743–1805), clergyman and theologian.

The next step in the argument is to note that design calls for a special kind of explanation. It is instructive to contrast a watch with, for example, a stone, as the 18th-century clergyman William Paley pointed out:

> *'In crossing a heath, suppose I pitched my foot against a stone, and were asked how the stone came to be there; I might possibly answer, that, for any thing I knew to the contrary, it had lain there for ever: nor would it perhaps be very easy to show the absurdity of this answer. But suppose I had found a*

watch upon the ground, and it should be inquired how the watch happened to be in that place; I should hardly think of the answer which I had before given, that, for any thing I knew, the watch might have always been there. Yet why should not this answer serve for the watch as well as for the stone? Why is it not as admissible in the second case, as in the first?[15]

The answer, of course, is that a watch is clearly designed for a specific purpose, while a stone is not. And such complex design, argued Paley, can only be the product of an intelligent designer. Watches do not just happen by chance; they are the product of human creativity. And in the same way, Paley concluded, animals and plants must be the product of some greater intelligence – a creator god.

This is a powerful argument, and it was not until Charles Darwin proposed his theory of evolution by natural selection in 1859 that its fundamental flaw was exposed. Paley's mistake, it turned out, was to assume that complex design can only be the product of an intelligent designer. That was a fair enough assumption before Darwin, because nobody could figure out any other way to explain the existence of design. This is what Darwin did; he described a purely physical mechanism by which complex design can emerge without the assistance of any intelligent designer. This is natural selection.

Natural selection works by the accumulation of tiny improvements. Offspring never resemble their parents exactly, and some of these differences may improve the offspring's survival chances. Perhaps a chick is born with a slightly harder beak, or a baby lizard with slightly better camouflage. These offspring will be more likely to reproduce and pass on the improvement to their offspring in turn. Over thousands of generations, the accumulation of many tiny improvements can add up to large changes, like a chain of Chinese whispers, with the descendants hardly resembling their distant ancestors at all. Fish evolve into amphibians, amphibians into monkeys, and monkeys into humans.

The mere possibility of natural selection blows Paley's argument to pieces. If complex design can evolve by a purely physical process, then animals and plants need not be the work of a creator god. When we also consider the fossil evidence, however, and the conservation of genetic sequences in different species, we are forced to conclude that natural selection is more than just a mere possibility; it is the only sensible explanation for the complex design we see all around us in nature.

This doesn't prove that gods *don't* exist. But in demolishing the main argument for their existence, it does pose a threat to those theists who think their beliefs can be justified rationally. Hence some Christians persist in looking for examples of design in nature that could not possibly have evolved by natural selection. If they can find just one such example, they argue, the argument from design will remain intact. The Christian biochemist Michael Behe has argued that the process of blood-clotting in vertebrates is too complex to have evolved by natural selection. His arguments have been demolished by other scientists, but his determination to look for more examples shows that he realizes how devastating the theory of natural selection is for Christian belief. What Behe fails to see, however, is how bizarre it would look if he did, in fact, manage to prove that blood-clotting could not have evolved. Think about it for a moment. What kind of god would go to such lengths to disguise his own handiwork and create a world that looks exactly like it had evolved entirely through natural selection, except for one or two microscopic biochemical pathways that require complex scientific equipment to discover? It would be a god who hid the proof of his existence like a needle in a giant haystack – a perverse, trickster god, completely unlike the kind, loving creator that Christians believe in.

Another argument that has played a crucial role in Christianity from the very beginning starts with a historical claim about the resurrection of Jesus. According to the gospels, Jesus died and his body was interred in a tomb, but a few days later the tomb was found empty. In the following weeks, several of his disciples thought they saw Jesus, and they came to believe that Jesus had risen from the dead. They concluded that their creator god must have brought Jesus back to life. Ergo, this god exists.

There are so many flaws in this shoddy piece of reasoning that it is hard to know where to begin. For one thing, it begs the question of why we should trust the gospels. After all, they are the work of believers, not of dispassionate observers. And the earliest of the four gospels – that of Mark – was not written down until at least 40 years after the death of Jesus, so there would have been more than enough time for the Chinese whispers of human remembering and retelling to transform perfectly normal events into magical wonders. Since the pioneering work of Sir Frederic Bartlett in the 1930s, psychologists have known that remembering does not involve retrieving an exact copy of the original experience but rather a process of imaginative reconstruction. This process is often biased by an unconscious tendency to reshape memories to fit well-worn narrative patterns. Sometimes whole chunks can be fabricated in a process that psychologists call confabulation.

Thomas Jefferson on the Bible

'... it is not to be understood that I am with him [Jesus] in all his doctrines. I am a Materialist; he takes the side of spiritualism. He preaches the efficacy of repentance toward forgiveness of sin; I require a counterpoise of good works to redeem it [...] Among the sayings & discourses imputed to him by his biographers, I find many passages of fine imagination, correct morality, and of the most lovely benevolence; and others again of so much ignorance, so much absurdity, so much untruth, charlatanism, and imposture, as to pronounce it impossible that such contradictions should have proceeded from the same being.'

Thomas Jefferson, in a letter to William Short, 13 April 1820.

The Christian response to such criticisms is to assert that the gospels are divinely inspired. That is, the creator god ensured that the human authors of the gospels only wrote down the unerring truth. However, this is of course a circular argument. It requires a prior belief in a god, and so it cannot then be used to prove the existence of that god. More worryingly, the gospels contradict each other on numerous points, and so some parts at least must be false. Textual criticism has also revealed many other indications that the gospels are normal products of fallible human beings, and not the infallible work of a creator god. As we will see in Chapter 3, the application of normal methods of historical and literary analysis to what believers regard as sacred scripture have proved to be threatening not just for Christians, but also to Muslims and Hindus.

This concludes our brief look at the role of reasoning in motivating belief and unbelief. It may appear to some that I have not given enough importance to this topic, and indeed other introductory works on atheism do tend to give greater prominence to arguments for and against the existence of gods. Much depends on the role one attributes to rationality in human thought in general. The relatively little space I have given to examining the arguments of either side here reflects my view that reason plays a much smaller role in human affairs than is generally thought.

3

The history of unbelief

There was a time when religion ruled the world. It is known as the Dark Ages.

Ruth Hurmence Green[16]

It's harder to trace the history of unbelief than the story of belief, since it is much less well documented, but this chapter makes a start by identifying some of the most important landmarks. I will describe some of the most famous atheists in history, and summarize their contributions to atheist thought. I will end by speculating about the likely future of religion and atheism in the next hundred years. Let us start at the very beginning, with the origins of humanity itself.

Anatomically, modern humans first appeared in Africa around 200,000 years ago. We don't know when they first started believing in gods, but there is some evidence that it was over 100,000 years ago. That is when the earliest known burial site has been dated to. Human remains from that time have been found in a cave in Israel stained with red ochre. A variety of grave goods were found at the burial site; the mandible of a wild boar, for example, was found in the arms of one of the skeletons. Other animals display only a casual interest in their dead, and the emergence of ritual burial thus represents a significant change in human behaviour. It suggests a belief in the afterlife, and an attendant belief in a spiritual realm, and possibly gods.

We can only imagine what these early forms of religion were like. Perhaps there was just a vague notion that powerful invisible beings existed who could help or harm humans. Perhaps these beings were nature spirits who inhabited sacred places like mountains, rivers and forests. Perhaps there were no especially religious people; everyone had equal access to the spirit world. Or perhaps one or two people were supposed to have

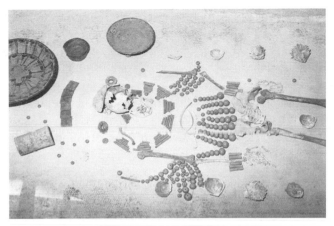

▲ A Mayan ritual burial with the deceased's belongings (grave goods) buried alongside them.

greater access; shamans and witch doctors, part-time holy men who acquired religious authority by means of their own charisma.

The first religions

When most people talk about religion today, they tend to have in mind the major contemporary world religions such as Christianity, Islam and Hinduism. But these hierarchical, organized religions have only been around for a few thousand years, and did not arise until humans started living in large cities with complex power structures. For the previous hundred thousand years, that is to say for the vast majority of human existence, people lived as hunter-gatherers in small nomadic bands. We know little about the religious practices of these groups, but they were certainly very different from the highly structured forms of religion that we observe today.

If there were any atheists in these bands of hunter-gatherers, they would probably have had a hard time. It is one thing to be an eccentric in a modern city with millions of people, and quite another to be one in a small, close-knit band in which survival depends on regular cooperation. Perhaps it never occurred to any of our hunter-gatherer ancestors to question the religious beliefs of their group. Or perhaps the few that did simply kept quiet.

The first recorded challenges to religious belief date from the sixth century BCE. Around that time in Ancient Greece, the philosopher Xenophanes pointed out how curious it was that most gods looked human and joked that if horses and cows had hands, then horses would draw the forms of gods like horses, and cows like cows. The idea that humans create gods in their own image, rather than the other way round, has since become a staple of atheist thinking.

When another Greek philosopher, Anaxagoras (fifth century BCE), claimed that the Sun was not a deity but simply a fiery mass, larger than the Peloponnese, a charge of impiety was brought against him, and he was forced to flee Athens. Soon after, the Atomists Leucippus and Democritus (fifth century BCE) produced the first fully materialistic philosophy, which explained the formation and development of the world in terms of the chance movements of atoms moving in infinite space.

Similar movements arose around the same time in India, where the Samkhya and Mimamsa schools of Hinduism rejected the idea of a creator deity. The Samkhya school believed in a dual existence of Prakriti ('nature') and Purusha ('spirit') but had no place for an Ishvara ('god') in its system, arguing that the existence of Ishvara cannot be proved and hence cannot be admitted to exist. Likewise, the Mimamsa school saw no need for an Ishvara in their system.

Despite these early developments, religious ideas continued to dominate every society around the world for the next 2,000 years. Religion has often played a critical role in legitimizing the social order, and anyone who questions it has therefore been perceived as a threat by those in power. In the 16th and 17th centuries CE it was still very dangerous to be an atheist. Étienne Dolet was strangled and burned for being an atheist in 1546, and Giulio Cesare Vanini met a similar fate in 1619.

Even with the advent of the Enlightenment in Europe in the 18th century, declarations of atheism still aroused hostility and public disapproval. When Baron d'Holbach published *The System of Nature* in 1770, he was forced to do so under a pseudonym, and the book was banned and publicly burned. French society was scandalized by the book's claim that the universe was nothing more than matter in motion, bound by inexorable natural laws of cause and effect. 'There is', wrote d'Holbach, 'no necessity to have recourse to supernatural powers to account for the formation of things.'[17]

The System of Nature has been called the first open denial of the existence of God and avowal of atheism since classical times, but it was not the only book to endorse a thoroughgoing materialism. Two decades beforehand,

L'Homme machine (*Man, a Machine*) caused outrage even in the relatively tolerant Netherlands, forcing its author to flee to Prussia. The man who had penned the book was Julien Offray de La Mettrie, a physician and philosopher who argued that not just the human body, but the human mind too, could be explained in purely mechanical terms. There was, in other words, no need to postulate the existence of a soul, a spiritual substance that outlived the body. This was perhaps even more threatening to Christian faith than d'Holbach's claim that the universe did not require a supernatural explanation.

In the following century, Karl Marx (1818–83) developed a sustained critique of religion on political lines, epitomized in his famous remark that religion is 'the opium of the people'[18]. Religion, in other words, is a soporific, a consolation designed to keep people quiet and prevent them from protesting against social injustice. Marx did not mean to imply that rulers consciously invented religions to maintain their power, although of course that cannot always be ruled out. But by drawing attention to the social effects of religious belief, Marx did highlight the way that belief in gods has often tended to legitimize existing power structures and dissuade people from challenging the authorities. It is noteworthy, for example, that the god portrayed in the Old Testament resembles nothing so much as a Middle Eastern monarch, demanding that homage be paid to him alone and crushing his enemies with extreme brutality. The implication is clear; if the very heavens embody such an order, then surely it is natural for society too.

Marx's attack on religion was echoed by another 19th-century German philosopher, Friedrich Nietzsche (1844–1900), who coined another famous aphorism: 'God is dead'. This is a deliberately provocative way of putting things, for strictly speaking neither theists nor atheists could agree with it; the god in which theists believe is supposed to be immortal, while atheists think that there never was any god to begin with. But Nietzsche did not intend the phrase to be taken literally; it was simply a poetic way of saying that belief in god was declining and religion was consequently losing its grip on society. Nietzsche saw this as a good thing, but it also presented a challenge, since religion had provided many people with a sense of purpose and meaning, and they would now have to face the consequences of the moral and spiritual gap left by god's absence.

By the year 1900, then, atheism was finally becoming a powerful force in the intellectual life of western societies. We have already seen how another 19th-century atheist, the biologist Charles Darwin, dealt what was perhaps the greatest ever body blow to theism when he proposed the theory of natural selection in 1859. Not long after, the poet Matthew Arnold found in the withdrawing ocean tide a metaphor for the retreat of religious faith, and heard in the water's sound a 'note of sadness'. In his poem 'Dover Beach', he lamented:

> The Sea of Faith
> Was once, too, at the full, and round earth's shore
> Lay like the folds of a bright girdle furl'd.
> But now I only hear
> Its melancholy, long, withdrawing roar,

Retreating, to the breath
Of the night-wind, down the vast edges drear
And naked shingles of the world.

▶ Breaking the spell of holy books

The 19th century also saw the application of scientific methods of textual analysis to the Bible, with devastating effect. Scholars such as David Strauss and Albert Schweitzer treated the gospels as ordinary historical documents, replete with errors, and attempted to unearth the nuggets of fact from the layers of myth and fantasy. Others established a chronology for the composition of the various books of the Bible and traced their sources to previous traditions. By encouraging a sceptical attitude to religious texts and treating them as historical documents like any other, the growth of biblical scholarship subtly but powerfully undermined Christian faith.

Holy books

Some believers treat their holy books fundamentally differently to the way they treat all other written texts. Christians believe the Bible is the result of divine inspiration. Muslims believe the Koran was dictated to Muhammad by an angel and will not even touch it unless they have first washed. Atheists believe all books are simply the product of human creativity and should all be treated with healthy scepticism.

Unfortunately, these advances in biblical scholarship have not yet been matched by equivalent developments in the history of other religions such as Islam and Hinduism. Our relatively primitive knowledge of Muhammad, for example, can be illustrated by contrasting his Wikipedia entry with that for Jesus. This is what Wikipedia has to say about Jesus:

> *'Virtually all modern scholars of antiquity agree that Jesus existed historically, although the quest for the historical Jesus has produced little agreement on the historical reliability of the Gospels and how closely the biblical Jesus reflects the historical Jesus. Most scholars agree that Jesus was a Jewish rabbi from Galilee who preached his message orally, was baptized by John the Baptist, and was crucified in Jerusalem on the orders of the Roman prefect, Pontius Pilate.'* [19]

Notice how this article is hedged about with caveats regarding the historical evidence and the differing levels of certainty about various aspects of Jesus' life. The use of phrases such as 'virtually all modern scholars of antiquity agree' and 'most scholars agree' continually reminds the reader not to take the biblical account at face value, but to treat it with the same scientific scrutiny as any other ancient text. Compare this with the Wikipedia entry on Muhammad:

> *'Born in about 570 CE in the Arabian city of Mecca, Muhammad was orphaned at an early age and brought up under the care of his paternal uncle Abu Talib. He later worked mostly as a merchant, as*

well as a shepherd, and was first married at age 25.
Being in the habit of periodically retreating to a cave
in the surrounding mountains for several nights of
seclusion and prayer, he later reported that it was
there, at age 40, that he was visited by Gabriel and
received his first revelation from God.'[20]

All the caveats are gone; the article uncritically repeats
the traditional Muslim account of Muhammad's life,
without any indication of how reliable the evidence
may be. And yet there are no extant biographies of
Muhammad before 750–800 CE, some *four to five*
generations after his death, while the first gospel was
written barely four decades after the death of Jesus,
i.e. within living memory. Despite the self-assured tone
of much writing about the life of Muhammad, then,
we actually know even less about him than we do about
the historical Jesus. It is certainly not at all clear that he
was born in Mecca, for example, nor that he worked as a
merchant, and it is highly unlikely that he was, as most
Muslims claim, illiterate.

Most of what Muslims believe about Muhammad, it now
seems, was invented wholesale or borrowed from the
accounts of other peoples' lives by Muslim rulers and
scholars around 150 to 200 years after the prophet's
death. And there were often powerful ideological motives
for these fabrications. The claim that Muhammad was
born in Mecca, for example, bolstered the legitimacy
of Abd Al-Malik, the fifth Umayyad Caliph, since it was
also the place of his birth. Yet many western accounts of
Muhammad's life continue to repeat unquestioningly the
traditional Muslim version.

The holy texts of Hinduism have likewise escaped the full force of historical scholarship, and when scholars do attempt to subject them to scientific scrutiny they face obstacles as fierce as those faced by the early critics of Christianity. Indian law, for example, makes it a criminal offence to publish a book that offends any Hindu, a law that jeopardizes the physical safety of any publisher, no matter how ludicrous the accusation brought against a book. In February 2014, Penguin India was forced to withdraw *The Hindus: An Alternative History* from the Indian market following an out-of-court settlement with Delhi-based complainants who had accused the book of 'distortion' aimed at 'denigrating Hindu traditions'. The author, Wendy Doniger, a leading scholar of Indian religious thought, has faced regular criticism from those who consider her work to be disrespectful of Hinduism in general. The complaints about her book alleged that she had 'hurt the religious feelings of millions of Hindus by declaring that the Ramayana is a fiction'. The Ramayana is one of the great Hindu epics and tells the story of how Rama (an avatar of the god Vishnu) rescues his wife Sita from Ravan, the king of Lanka. The critics objected to Doniger 'placing the Ramayana in its historical context' and thereby demonstrating 'that it is a work of fiction, created by human authors'.

▶ The end of religion?

Many 19th-century thinkers assumed that religion would eventually disappear altogether. They argued that the gradual process of secularization, whereby religious creeds, practices and institutions gradually lose their social significance, would culminate in a world based on science and reason. The sociologist Max Weber called this process the 'disenchantment of the world[21]', a phrase which indicates some ambivalence; Weber saw secularization as both freeing humans from old-fashioned prejudices and robbing the world of some of its magic.

The secularization thesis was bolstered by the appearance in the 20th century of the world's first atheist states. After the Russian Revolution of 1917, the Soviet Union banned religion, confiscated religious property and propagated atheism in schools. With the establishment of the People's Republic of China in 1949, atheism became official there too, although religious persecution did not reach its full force until the Cultural Revolution of 1966–7, when thousands of places of worship were destroyed.

Durkheim on secularization

'Thus there is something eternal in religion that is destined to outlive the succession of particular symbols in which religious thought has clothed itself. [...] In short, the former gods are growing old or dying, and others have not been born [...] A day will come when our societies once again will know hours of creative effervescence during which new ideas will again spring forth and new formulas emerge to guide humanity for a time.'

Émile Durkheim, *The Elementary Forms of Religious Life* (1912)

Towards the end of the 20th century, however, there were signs that the tide might be turning and religion staging a comeback. The Iranian revolution of 1979 overthrew the western-backed monarchy and replaced it with an Islamic republic ruled by a religious leader, the Ayatollah Khomeini. A decade later, the collapse of the Soviet Union led to a return of religious and ethnic conflict in the Balkans, with the Serbs helped by Christian fighters from Russia and the Bosnians receiving support from Muslim groups, including fighters from the Lebanese guerrilla organization Hezbollah. In the 1990s, the Middle East saw the rise of terrorist groups like Al-Qaeda committing atrocities in the name of a radical form of Islam.

In the west, a wide range of alternative religious movements sprang up to fill the vacuum left by the retreat of Christianity. Interest in Hindu spirituality grew in the 1960s, as a number of influential Indian teachers of yoga attracted followers in the United States and Europe. In 1978 over 900 members of the Peoples Temple, a cult led by the charismatic preacher Jim Jones, committed mass suicide in Jonestown, Guyana. In 1995, members of a Japanese cult called Aum Shinrikyo released poison gas on several lines of the Tokyo subway, killing 13 people and injuring many others. Two years after that, 39 members of an American cult called Heaven's Gate committed mass suicide in California in the belief that they would join an alien spacecraft.

On the other hand, the number of people in the world claiming to be religious fell by 9 per cent from 2005 to 2011, while the number of people identifying themselves as atheists rose by 3 per cent. The picture is a mixed one, therefore, and the philosopher Jürgen Habermas has argued that we are witnessing the rise of 'post-secular' societies, in which many belief systems, some religious and some not, compete for followers.

Given this complexity, it is hard to predict what the future holds for atheism and religion. The philosopher Daniel Dennett has sketched out five possible scenarios:

▶ The enlightenment is long gone. The creeping 'secularization' of modern societies that has been anticipated for two centuries is evaporating before our eyes.

▶ Religion is in its death throes. Today's outbursts of fervour and fanaticism are but a brief and awkward transition to a truly modern society in which religion plays at most a ceremonial role.

▶ Religions transform themselves into institutions unlike anything seen before on the planet: basically creedless associations selling self-help and enabling moral teamwork, using ceremony and tradition to cement relationships and build 'long-term fan loyalty'.

▶ Religion diminishes in prestige and visibility, rather like smoking. It is tolerated, since there are those who say they can't live without it, but it is discouraged, and teaching religion to impressionable young children is frowned upon in most societies and actually outlawed in others.

▶ Judgement Day arrives. The blessed ascend bodily into heaven, and the rest are left behind to suffer the agonies of the damned, as the Antichrist is vanquished.

The last scenario is deliberately whimsical. Dennett includes it in his list partly because, as a philosopher, he cannot rule it out completely on purely logical grounds, and partly because it is what many millions of people still believe. His five scenarios are not meant to be exhaustive, but simply to illustrate that the stark opposition between secularization and re-enchantment is too simplistic to capture the full range of possibilities. One thing is clear, however; the idea that society is progressing steadily towards an ever more rational future, in which religion will inevitably disappear, has turned out to be as much of a myth as the stories of Zeus and Odin.

4

The psychology of belief

Any time I see a person fleeing from reason and into religion, I think to myself: There goes a person who simply cannot stand being so goddamned lonely anymore.

Kurt Vonnegut[22]

If gods don't exist, then why has belief in their existence been so prevalent throughout history, and why do the vast majority of people continue to believe in them? An error so popular and persistent demands explanation.

The standard scientific explanation for a biological phenomenon as widespread as theism is natural selection. Almost every human being grows up learning to speak a language, and biologists explain this ubiquity by postulating an innate 'language instinct' that has evolved because it gave our ancestors an advantage over those who lacked it. But it seems odd to explain the prevalence of theism in the same way, since it is hard to imagine how it could be advantageous to believe in something that doesn't exist. Hence, most evolutionary psychologists have concluded that belief in gods is a by-product of cognitive processes and behaviours that evolved for unrelated reasons. In this chapter I will describe some of these cognitive processes, and show how a belief in gods might well result as a purely fortuitous and unintended consequence of their interaction.

Psychological research has identified certain systematic patterns of error that affect the human mind. One way of categorizing types of error is to divide them into two groups: false positives (in which x is mistakenly identified as y), and false negatives (in which x is not recognized as y, even though it is). Psychologists have identified many cognitive systems in which these errors are not randomly distributed but systematically skewed in one direction. In other words, instead of making an equal number of each type of mistake, many cognitive systems make more of one kind than the other. For example, the psychological mechanisms responsible for spotting patterns are biased towards false positives: they are more likely to see a pattern in what is, in fact, entirely random than to mistake order for chaos. A classic example is the so-called 'clustering effect', which makes people more likely to mistake a random sequence of coin tosses for a non-random one than vice versa.

Cognitive biases and free will

It is interesting that cognitive biases tend to predispose people to believe in gods; no cognitive bias favours atheism. It thus appears that children are 'cognitively prepared' for belief, even before they are capable of understanding the complex ideas of any given religion. This poses a serious challenge to the Christian notion that the creator has left his creatures free to disbelieve. A Christian who accepts the evidence from psychology would have to concede that, on the contrary, the creator has endowed the human mind with a strong innate tendency to believe in him. It would appear that the creator has heavily loaded the dice in his favour.

Experimental evidence suggests that there is a similar bias in the psychological mechanisms for spotting causal relations and intentional agents. That is, we are more likely to imagine that things are causally related when they are not than vice versa, and more likely to see an intentional agent where there is none than fail to spot one that is there. Several psychologists and anthropologists have argued that these cognitive biases provide a naturalistic explanation for the origin of many religious beliefs. The psychologist B. F. Skinner, for example, argued that the tendency to see causal relations where there are none, which is also evident in non-human animals, was at the root of many superstitions. In a famous experiment, Skinner placed hungry pigeons in cages fitted with automatic mechanisms which delivered food to the pigeons 'at regular intervals with no reference whatsoever to the bird's behaviour'. He found that the pigeons associated the delivery of the food with whatever chance actions they had been performing as it was delivered, and that they subsequently continued to perform these same actions:

'One bird was conditioned to turn counter-clockwise about the cage, making two or three turns between reinforcements. Another repeatedly thrust its head into one of the upper corners of the cage. A third developed a "tossing" response, as if placing its head beneath an invisible bar and lifting it repeatedly. Two birds developed a pendulum motion of the head and body, in which the head was extended forward and swung from right to left with a sharp movement followed by a somewhat slower return.'[23]

Skinner suggested that the pigeons behaved as if they were influencing the automatic mechanism with their rituals and that this experiment shed light on human behaviour:

'The experiment might be said to demonstrate a sort of superstition. The bird behaves as if there were a causal relation between its behaviour and the presentation of food, although such a relation *is lacking. There are many analogies in human behaviour. Rituals for changing one's fortune at cards are good examples. A few accidental connections between a ritual and favourable consequences suffice to set up and maintain the behaviour in spite of many unreinforced instances. The bowler who has released a ball down the alley but continues to behave as if she were controlling it by twisting and turning her arm and shoulder is another case in point. These behaviours have, of course, no real effect upon one's luck or upon a ball half way down an alley, just as in the present case the food would appear as often if the pigeon did nothing – or, more strictly speaking, did something else.'[24]*

Superstition might then be a natural result of a 'hyperactive causation detector'. In a similar way, the anthropologists Scott Atran and Pascal Boyer have argued that beliefs in spirits and gods may be a natural result of a parallel tendency to mistake inanimate things for intentional agents. Justin Barrett attributes this tendency to what he calls a 'hyperactive agent detection device'[25], or HADD; it is 'hyperactive' because it sometimes leads us to attribute agency to non-living things such as thunder and lightning. The HADD led our ancestors to see these dramatic natural phenomena as the actions of powerful superhuman beings, rather than as simple physical processes.

Why did these cognitive biases evolve in the first place? Surely, you might think, natural selection would favour a mind that makes as few errors as possible? That is true, but it also matters what *kinds* of error the mind makes. Even the most acute mind will make some mistakes, and if some errors are more costly than others, it will pay to have a mind that is biased in favour of making the less costly errors. And in many evolutionary contexts, it is certainly the case that some errors are far more costly than others. When it comes to detecting predators, false positives are much less costly than false negatives; far better to mistake a stick for a snake than vice versa. Likewise, when it comes to spotting causal relations, it is better to end up with a few useless superstitions than to miss the rare but valuable genuine causal pattern. Cognitive systems for detecting predators and causal relations should, therefore, evolve to err on the side of making more false positives than false negatives, rather than an equal number of each type of mistake.

It is easy to see how these cognitive biases could give rise to belief in gods. The tendency to perceive agency in non-living things could lie behind the animism that forms the world-view of tribal peoples, in which every river, every forest, every mountain is the home to some god. Likewise, the tendency to see causal relations where there are none could have led our ancestors to say prayers to these imaginary deities in the hope that the sun would continue to rise and the rain continue to fall. Religion would have evolved, then, as a by-product of cognitive biases that evolved separately and for completely non-religious reasons. Thus an evolutionary account does not presuppose that religious belief played any direct role in increasing the survival chances of our ancestors.

Cognitive biases can also shed light on cases of pareidolia, in which people perceive imagery in natural phenomena. In 1978, for example, a New Mexican woman found that the burn marks on a tortilla she had made appeared similar to the traditional western depiction of Jesus's face. Thousands of people subsequently came to see the

▲ The stump of a willow tree in Rathkeale, Ireland, in which observers claimed to see the silhouette of the Virgin Mary.

framed tortilla. In 2009, a similarly abundant number of Irish Catholics flocked to a church in Rathkeale, County Limerick, to pray at the stump of a recently cut willow tree in which many observers claimed to see the silhouette of the Virgin Mary. It would appear that the cognitive mechanisms responsible for face recognition are just as prone to false positives as the mechanisms for spotting causal relations and intentional agents.

There is nothing inherently atheistic about subjecting religious experience to the same scientific scrutiny as any other natural phenomenon. As the pioneer in this endeavour, William James, was careful to state in his lectures on natural theology, published in *The Varieties of Religious Experience* (1902), studying religion as a natural phenomenon is quite possible without taking any view on whether or not religion is also a supernatural phenomenon. Nevertheless, both believers and non-believers have tended to feel that by shining a harsh light on the often prosaic nature of religious experience, psychological research cannot help but cast doubt on its supposed supernatural aspects. Indeed, this may be why Christians have often resisted scientific scrutiny of their beliefs; as Daniel Dennett observes, 'the religious ... often bristle at the impertinence, the lack of respect, the *sacrilege*, implied by anybody who wants to investigate their views'[26]. Dennett suggests that this 'taboo against a forthright, no-holds-barred scientific investigation of one natural phenomenon among many' is bound together with religion itself in a 'curious embrace'[27]. Part of the strength of religion itself may be due to the protection it receives from this taboo.

▶ Why do atheists exist?

If belief in gods really is a by-product of universal cognitive biases that evolved for other reasons, it would certainly explain why theism has been so prevalent throughout history and why it remains so common today. It would, however, make it hard to understand why there are any atheists. If the cognitive biases that give rise to religious belief are innate and universal, how is that anyone manages to overcome them?

The answer lies in another fundamental fact of biology – namely, that no two animals are exactly alike. Although the cognitive biases that underlie belief in gods are found in everyone, they vary in strength. Some people, in other words, are more prone to these biases than others. Take the tendency to perceive faces in random patterns, for example. In a particularly revealing experiment carried out by Peter Brugger, a neurologist at the University Hospital in Zurich, volunteers were asked to distinguish real faces from scrambled faces as the images were flashed up briefly on a screen, and then to distinguish real words from made-up ones. Those who believed in the paranormal were much more likely than sceptics to see a word or face when there wasn't one, whereas sceptics were more likely to miss real faces and words when they appeared on the screen.

The researchers then gave the volunteers a drug called L-dopa, which is usually used to relieve the symptoms of Parkinson's disease by increasing levels of dopamine in the brain. Under the influence of the drug, both groups made more mistakes, but the sceptics became less likely to miss the faces and words when they were scrambled. This suggests that paranormal thoughts are associated with high levels of dopamine in the brain, and the L-dopa makes sceptics less sceptical.

More generally, people with higher levels of dopamine are more likely to find significance in coincidences and pick out meaning and patterns where there are none. Perhaps the difference between believers and atheists boils down largely to how much dopamine they are born with. This would certainly be consistent with the dopamine hypothesis of schizophrenia, according to which some of the symptoms of disease are caused by hyperactive dopaminergic signal transduction; paranoid delusions often involve the attribution of sinister meanings to random events such as lottery numbers or freak accidents.

Another symptom of schizophrenia which may be caused by high levels of dopamine in the brain is hallucination. Psychologists now think that hallucinations are more common than was previously suspected, and are by no means limited to schizophrenics. Indeed, there seems to be a continuum from the bizarre visions of the latter to the almost imperceptible illusions which are common features of everyday life. Reports of religious statues nodding should not be taken at face value, therefore, even if the observers are not mad. Indeed, the disciples of Jesus may have hallucinated some of the more bizarre episodes recounted in the gospels, such as the ascent of Jesus into heaven, without necessarily suffering from full-blown schizophrenia.

Mystical experiences

According to the psychologist William James, mystical experiences have four defining qualities:

Ineffability: the mystical experience 'defies expression, that no adequate report of its content can be given in words'.

Noetic quality: mystics stress that their experiences give them 'insight into depths of truth unplumbed by the discursive intellect'.

Transiency: most mystical experiences have a short occurrence, but their effect persists.

Passivity: mystics come to their peak experience not as active seekers, but as passive recipients.

These findings suggest that the brains of believers and atheists may be different in some fundamental way, or at least that certain brain chemicals may predispose a person to being religious, while lack of them may lead in the opposite direction. This fits well with a funny experiment that Richard Dawkins conducted in 2003. The neuroscientist Michael Persinger had constructed an electronic headset that he claimed caused many people to report 'mystical experiences and altered states' when wearing it. Intrigued, Dawkins decided to give it a try; 'I've always been curious to know what it would be like to have a mystical experience,' he told reporters before the experiment[20]. The result? Nothing. After wearing the so-called 'god helmet' for some time, all Dawkins reported was a slight feeling of dizziness. And his legs twitched a little.

Perhaps Dawkins is so utterly lacking in whatever brain chemicals predispose people to believing in gods that even Persinger's high-tech gizmo couldn't elicit the feelings that come so naturally to believers. Maybe his brain sits at one extreme of a continuum, with mystics and madmen at the other. That doesn't mean all atheists are similarly 'tone-deaf'. Brain chemistry is not destiny, and there are many routes to unbelief. My brain, for example, is clearly wired up very differently to that of Dawkins, since I have had several mystical experiences, and without the aid of any god helmet, although psychedelic drugs may have been instrumental in one or two. Perhaps these differences in brain chemistry may also help to explain the different attitudes that atheists adopt towards religion, which we will examine in Chapter 5.

▶ The psychology of cult leaders

As well as throwing light on the origins of religion, and the reasons why most (but not all) people believe in gods, psychology can also throw light on the personality of those who have founded new religions. Several of the great world religions started off as small cults led by charismatic individuals. The Buddha, Moses, Jesus and Muhammad were all probably real historical figures with similar psychological traits. Like modern cult leaders, such as Jim Jones and Sun Yung Moon, they all believed they had a special mission and had some special insight into the nature of reality.

Cults vs 'new religious movements'

Most sociologists and scholars of religion no longer talk about 'cults' because of the word's negative connotations. Instead they tend to use other terms such as 'new religious movements' and 'alternative religions' to describe most of the groups that had previously been described as cults. However, none of these new terms has had much success in popular culture or in the media. Moreover, they beg the question by assuming that all cults are religious phenomena, when in fact there are also secular and atheist cults.

We can only speculate how these figures came to believe they were so special. Take Jesus, for example. Jesus' miracles were entirely typical of the conjuring tricks that were popular around the Mediterranean in the first century CE. Hippolytus, for example, describes a certain Marcus who had mastered the art of turning the water in a cup red by mixing liquid from another cup while the onlookers' attention was distracted. The psychologist Nicholas Humphrey has suggested that, even though Jesus was regularly using deception and trickery in his public performances like any other conjuror, he came to believe that he was something more – that sometimes he could genuinely exert the powers he claimed. Humphrey points out that many faith healers start off with deliberate deception, employing methods that they know full well to be tricks. As their reputation grows, however, and they gather followers, they gradually come to believe their own lies, and eventually become capable of breathtaking doublethink.[29]

Humphrey's speculations on the psychology of Jesus are just that – speculations. Nevertheless, they do provide a plausible account of how a normal, fallible human being like Jesus might come to believe he was the Messiah and Son of God. It must have been dreadful when, in the final moments of his life, as he hung from the cross, he found he could not summon up any supernatural help when he most needed it. That would suggest a rather different kind of pathos in those famous words attributed to Jesus in his last moments, echoing Psalm 22: 'My God, my God, why hast thou forsaken me?' If Jesus really did say something like this as he was dying, then those words might express genuine bewilderment on his part that the wonderful destiny he had imagined for himself had failed to materialize.

In the case of Muhammad, things are somewhat different. There is no sign in the gospels that Jesus ever hallucinated, but it seems clear that Muhammad heard voices on a regular basis and saw angels. The most likely explanation is that he suffered from schizophrenia. For most of human history, mental illness was seen as something supernatural, either divine or demonic, and in the superstitious atmosphere of seventh-century Arabia, Muhammad's hallucinations were seen as signs from a god. Today he would be treated in a psychiatric hospital.

Most cults do not survive the death of their founders. When they do, as was the case with Christianity and Islam, the charismatic authority of the founder is inherited and transformed by a bureaucracy in a process that Max Weber termed 'the routinization of charisma'.

This bureaucracy may become so wealthy and powerful that, as with the Roman Catholic Church today, it is hard to imagine how it could have originated in a weird cult with just a few, poor members. Viewed as purely historical phenomena, Christianity and Islam must rank among the most successful start-ups in history.

Perhaps the most famous cult to emerge in recent times was the so-called Peoples Temple. Founded in Indiana in 1955 by a young civil rights activist called Jim Jones, by the mid-1970s it had spread to over a dozen locations in California and moved its headquarters to San Francisco. In 1974, the Peoples Temple signed a lease to rent land in Guyana where they would build a socialist paradise called Jonestown. Jones himself moved there in 1977 and encouraged other Temple members to follow him. Within a year, the population had grown to over 900 people.

In November 1978, a US Congressman called Leo Ryan visited Jonestown to investigate claims of abuse within the Peoples Temple. While he was there a number of Temple members told Ryan that they wanted to return to the United States, and accompanied him to a nearby airstrip where a plane was waiting. As they were boarding the plane, some Temple security guards arrived and opened fire on the group, killing the Congressman, three journalists and one of the Temple defectors. That evening, Jones ordered his congregation to drink a potent mix of cyanide, sedatives and powdered fruit juice. Parents were instructed to administer the poison to their young children. The mass suicide and killings at Jonestown were the greatest single loss of

▲ The aftermath of the mass suicide and killings at Jonestown, Guyana, in 1978, when members of Peoples Temple drank a cyanide cocktail.

American civilian life in a deliberate act until the events of 11 September 2001.

But the Peoples Temple was an atheist cult, not a religious one. Although Jim Jones started off as a Pentecostalist preacher, he soon became sceptical of the Bible and told his closest followers that he was just using religion as a means to advance the cause of socialism. If there was a god, it was Jones himself, who claimed to come from the 'ether plane' and to know everything. He spoke of death, vaguely, as 'passing over to the other side', but he didn't offer any hope of heaven or life after death. Drinking the poison, he said, was not a religious sacrifice but an act of 'revolutionary suicide', a gesture of resistance against the capitalist mercenaries and the CIA, who were determined to wipe out the Temple.

The danger of people like Jim Jones and Jesus, then, lies not so much in what they preach as in the charismatic authority they wield. Whether in the name of gods or secular ideals, cult leaders use psychological techniques to gain immense power over their followers, inducing in them a debilitating sense of dependence on the leader and dulling their critical faculties. Atheists can be just as vulnerable to such influence as believers, especially if they consider themselves above such things. We must all be alert against demagogues and charlatans, whether they come in the name of religion or not.

5

Atheism and religion

Religion. It's given people hope in a world torn apart by religion.

Jon Stewart, The Daily Show

All atheists agree that religions are human creations and gods mere figments of the imagination. But beyond this shared perspective, atheists take a variety of different approaches to religion. Some see it as a dangerous social phenomenon that should be eliminated, while others think there may be much of value that atheists can salvage from its many and varied achievements. In this chapter I will describe some of these different perspectives and offer my own suggestion about how atheists should treat religion.

There is a short story by the Marquis de Sade in which a priest comes to a dying atheist to give him the last rites. Instead of meekly confessing his sins, however, the atheist uses his final moments to argue with the priest about god:

> 'Put away your prejudices, unbend, be a man, be human, without fear and without hope forget your gods and your religions too: they are none of them good for anything but to set man at odds with man, and the mere name of these horrors has caused greater loss of life on earth than all other wars and all other plagues combined.'[30]

Finally, the dying man confesses that he has prepared a final pleasure to enjoy before he perishes; 'six women lovelier than the light of day are waiting in the chamber adjoining,' he reveals, and invites the priest to 'partake of the feast with me, following my example embrace them instead of the vain sophistries of superstition, under their caresses strive for a little while to forget your hypocritical beliefs'. The dying man rings a bell, the women come in to the room, and the priest abandons his faith and joins in the orgy.

One senses that the pleasure of robbing the priest of his faith was perhaps more dear to this dying man than his final fornication. And the same desire to convert religious people to unbelief seems to pervade the writings of some contemporary atheists, such as Richard Dawkins and Sam Harris. Indeed, their attacks on religion are so vitriolic and bad-tempered as to alienate the sensitive reader and give atheism a bad name. Dawkins has even gone so far as to compare religious education to child abuse. I sometimes think that no other atheist has done more for the cause of religion than Richard Dawkins.

Atheist proselytism

Proselytism is the act of persuading people to accept your beliefs. It usually refers to the attempt of believers to convert people to their religion, but it can in principle refer to any attempt to convert people to a different point of view, religious or not. Atheists who try to persuade believers that there are no gods are therefore engaging in a kind of proselytism themselves.

The New Atheism, as this more aggressive strand has sometimes been dubbed, can at times seem like a kind of 'secular fundamentalism'. Even when atheists take a more humorous approach to promoting their message, such proselytism is still reminiscent of missionaries trying to convert others to their religion. In 2009, a campaign organized by the British Humanist Association in collaboration with Richard Dawkins, aimed to place 'peaceful and upbeat' messages about atheism on transport media in Britain in response to evangelical Christian advertising. Several hundred buses around the UK were adorned with the slogan: 'There's probably no God. Now stop worrying and enjoy your life'. Don't be fooled by the lighthearted tone; this is still preaching. And this strikes me as quite ironic, for it suggests, let's say, a certain *insecurity*; those who are truly comfortable in their atheism feel no need to inflict it on others.

▲ Campaign creator Ariane Sherine and Richard Dawkins at the launch of the atheist bus poster campaign in London in 2009.

Let me be clear; I am not endorsing the dreadful notion that somehow 'all beliefs are equal', or that 'everybody has their own truth'. There are objective truths, and when I say that I'm atheist, I mean that I believe there really are no gods. Consequently, I think that anyone who believes in gods must be mistaken. But I really can't be bothered to argue with them about it, let alone try and convince them to become atheists like me. For one thing, I would be unlikely to succeed; people rarely change their minds through rational argument. But more importantly, I don't really care what other people think. If someone else wrongly believes in the existence of gods and devils, that's their problem, not mine. I've got better things to do than waste my time and energy enlightening them.

Some of my fellow atheists might object that while I might not care what other people think, there are some people who seem to care a lot what I think. Some Muslim fundamentalists, for example, might see my atheism as a crime against their god and seek to harm me if I express my views openly or say anything that contradicts their creed. As we saw in Chapter 1, atheists still suffer from prejudice and persecution in many countries around the world, and if we wish to protect them it is incumbent upon us to rid the world of the dangerous beliefs that animate their enemies.

This argument does not convince me. It is the *actions* of these bigots that must be changed, not their thoughts. Of course their religious beliefs play a part in driving their actions, but not a decisive one. Many of those who share the same religious beliefs do not engage in persecution or violence. Perhaps fear stops them, or perhaps laziness – it doesn't really matter. All that really counts is that they don't murder or persecute people with different beliefs. What separates these harmless believers from their dangerous co-religionists is unclear; in addition to, or perhaps regardless of, the beliefs they share, other, darker psychological forces that have little or nothing to do with religion are required to trigger actual violence. We must be careful to distinguish between thoughts and deeds. People can think what they like providing they don't engage in destructive or unethical actions.

Some atheists may think they have a duty to disabuse believers of their errors and enlighten them as to the true nature of reality. But theists are equally convinced that it is they who are in possession of the truth, and moreover are often enjoined by their religion to enlighten others. The result is, then, a clash of opposing beliefs, as each side attempts to convince the other of their version of the truth. Yet it seems particularly perverse for atheists to engage in the kind of doctrinal squabble that has been such a salient feature of the history of religion. Surely atheists can highlight the superiority of their belief system more efficiently by abstaining from proselytism than by engaging in it. It is beneath our dignity to jump into the muddy pit where the believers slug it out. Don't wrestle with a pig, the saying goes; you both get dirty, but the pig enjoys it.

▶ Valuing religion

Not all atheists see religion as a dangerous social phenomenon that should be eliminated; some find something of value in religious traditions. The philosopher Alain de Botton, for example, suggests that such traditions are packed with good ideas that atheists can steal. In his book *Religion for Atheists*, he argues that religions contain valuable insights in building communities and making relationships last, as well as teaching us how to overcome feelings of envy and inadequacy, and how to appreciate art, architecture and music.

It should probably be clear by now that my sympathies lie more with Alain de Botton than with Richard Dawkins. I think atheists can find something of value in many religious traditions. As Daniel Dennett points out, religions have accumulated thousands of years of 'R&D' in constructing social institutions, meditative practices and moral experiments that atheists can learn from. Certainly, many religious practices and inventions are of dubious value, and some outright pernicious, so discretion must be applied when sifting the wheat from the chaff. But it is hard to deny that religions can present potent metaphors and images to represent human aspirations for transcendence. And whatever else they may be, religions are surely testimony to the creativity and power of the human imagination. Think of all those wonderful stories in the Old Testament, or the Greek myths, or the legends of Odin and Thor. Then there are the powerful epics of Hindu literature and the beautiful temple carvings in Mexico. To immerse oneself in these creations is to enter an exciting parallel universe that can at times make the secular one seem quite drab by comparison.

Many atheists would disagree. Religious art leaves them cold, and they tend to highlight its less appealing features – the representations of human sacrifice

▲ Detail of the depiction of the Mesoamerican deity Quetzalcoatl ('feathered serpent'), at the Temple of Quetzalcoatl in Teotihuacan, once the largest city in the pre-Columbian Americas and now a UNESCO World Heritage Site near present-day Mexico City.

'We have grown frightened of the word morality. We bridle at the thought of hearing a sermon. We flee from the idea that art should be uplifting or have an ethical mission. We don't go on pilgrimages. We can't build temples. We have no mechanisms for expressing gratitude. Strangers rarely sing together. We are presented with an unpleasant choice between either committing to peculiar concepts about immaterial deities or letting go entirely of a host of consoling, subtle or just charming rituals for which we struggle to find equivalents in secular society.'

Alain de Botton, *Religion for Atheists: A Non-believer's Guide to the Uses of Religion* (2012)

on Mexican temples, for example, or the remarkably childish nature of the squabbles on Mount Olympus. The sociologist Frank Furedi notes that these atheists get particularly worked up about religious films such as Mel Gibson's *The Passion of the Christ*, or allegories like *The Lion, The Witch and The Wardrobe*. But Furedi himself seems to fall prey to the same failure of imagination when he writes that 'in Gibson's vision Jesus is reduced to little more than a lump of meat, the victim of whippings and abuse whose physical suffering is shown in gruesome detail. It is far from uplifting.'[31] Such a description betrays the purely secular viewpoint from which Furedi is writing. I too reacted in a similar way when I first saw the film. Indeed, I had to stop the DVD at the point where Jesus was being whipped as I could not bear to see such bloody violence. It seemed so gratuitous, and it felt wrong to watch a man being tortured.

But then I realized that, to a Christian viewer, this was not simply 'a man being tortured'. To a Christian, this was the Son of God, suffering to redeem our sins. And I recalled what that great humanist David Hume had to say about appreciating works of art:

> 'We may observe, that every work of art, in order to produce its due effect on the mind, must be surveyed in a certain point of view, and not be fully relished by persons, whose situation, real or imaginary, is not conformable to that which is required by the performance.'[32]

In viewing Gibson's film from my own, secular viewpoint, I had been like the man who, in Hume's words, 'obstinately maintains his natural position, without placing himself in that point of view, which the performance supposes'[33]. Hume condemns this lack of imagination in no uncertain terms:

> 'If the work be addressed to persons of a different age or nation, he makes no allowance for their peculiar views and prejudices; but, full of the manners of his own age and country, rashly condemns what seemed admirable in the eyes of those for whom alone the discourse was calculated. ... By this means, his sentiments are perverted; nor have the same beauties and blemishes the same influence upon him, as if he had imposed a proper violence on his imagination, and had forgotten himself for a moment. So far his taste evidently departs from the

true standard; and of consequence loses all credit and authority. [34]

Hume is particularly keen to point out the relevance of such a principle to religious art:

'On this account, all the absurdities of the pagan system of theology must be overlooked by every critic, who would pretend to form a just notion of ancient poetry; and our posterity, in their turn, must have the same indulgence to their forefathers. No religious principles can ever be imputed as a fault to any poet.' [35]

So, taking Hume at his word, I proceeded to watch *The Passion of the Christ* again from the beginning, and to 'impose a proper violence on my imagination' while doing so. I endeavoured, that is, to see it from a Christian point of view. It was quite hard at first. But as I grew accustomed to this alien perspective, the film began to affect me in a completely different way. With my Christian hat on, so to speak, I no longer saw a pointless act of torture but a beautiful act of redemption. And instead of feeling repelled by the brutality, I was moved to tears by this act of divine love.

The experience did not turn me back into a Christian. When the film ended (for I saw it through to the end this time), I took off my Christian hat and put my atheist one back on. But I had gained something in that temporary holiday from my own belief system. I had become aware of how different things seem from a religious point of view. I often wish more of my fellow atheists would try to do the same.

▶ Religious education

If there is one religious activity above all that makes many atheists bristle, it is religious education. Preach all you want, they might argue, to adults who can challenge what you say and meet you on equal terms; but do not impose your religious views on young children, whose minds are so impressionable. And yet many religions have laid great emphasis on the instruction of young children precisely because they are so easy to influence. As the Jesuit founder St Ignatius of Loyola is supposed to have observed: 'Give me a child until he is seven and I will show you the man'.

Freedom of education

Freedom of education is the right for parents to have their children educated in accordance with their religious and other views. It is a legal principle that has been enshrined in the European Convention on Human Rights and in several national constitutions, such as the Belgian constitution and the Dutch constitution. Some atheists oppose this principle because they think teaching religion to children is akin to indoctrination. The biggest arguments concern state-funded education. Some people oppose religious education in public schools because it constitutes state sponsorship of the religious beliefs being taught.

Parents in the United States have the legal right to educate their children entirely at home if they wish, and nearly one million families do so. Others send their children to sectarian schools that are permitted to teach subjects in whatever way they choose, which often means presenting information only from a biblical point of view. The neuroscientist and atheist Nicholas Humphrey has argued that this is immoral, and that parents and schools should be *forbidden by law* from teaching their children to believe in the literal truth of the Bible:

> '... *children have a right not to have their minds addled by nonsense. And we as a society have a duty to protect them from it. So we should no more allow parents to teach their children to believe, for example, in the literal truth of the Bible, or that the planets rule their lives, than we should allow parents to knock their children's teeth out or lock them in a dungeon.'* [36]

Humphrey's motives for putting forward this radical proposal are entirely benign; he wants to ensure that people remain open to new opportunities of learning throughout their lives and not have their critical faculties stunted in childhood. Yet by calling for the power of the state to be used to enforce his views, he betrays an authoritarian leaning that smacks once again of the ideological totalism we first discussed in Chapter 2. To recap, ideological totalism is the conviction that there is just one path to true existence, just one valid mode of being, and that all others are therefore invalid and false. There are secular kinds of totalism too, but it seems clear that religions – particularly monotheistic religions – have a much more intimate association with totalism, at least in the west. It would seem particularly ironic, not to say perverse, for atheists to pursue their own form of totalism. And anyone who wishes to co-opt the power of the state to prevent the teaching of ideas he disagrees with is clearly a totalist of the most dangerous kind.

▶ Atheistic apathy

While Dawkins and de Botton take very different attitudes to religion, they have one thing in common; they both care about it a great deal. But there is a third kind of atheist, who neither hates religion nor finds anything of value in it; he simply doesn't care. In *The Outsider* by Albert Camus, the protagonist Mersault repeatedly refuses to see the prison chaplain as he awaits his execution. Finally, the priest visits him anyway:

> '"Why do you refuse to see me?" he said. I replied that I didn't believe in God. He wanted to know whether I was quite sure about that and I said I had no reason for asking myself that question: it didn't seem to matter. He then lent back against the wall, with his hands flat on his thighs. Almost as if he were talking to himself, he remarked that sometimes you think you're sure when really you're not. I didn't say anything. He looked at me and asked, "What do you think?" I replied that it was possible. In any case, I may not have been sure what really interested me, but I was absolutely sure what didn't interest me. And what he was talking about was one of the very things that didn't interest me.'[37]

This seems to be the attitude that Neill deGrasse Tyson was trying to strike in the passage I quoted in Chapter 1, where he rather clumsily tried to distance himself from the word *atheist*. 'Atheists I know who proudly wear the badge,' he continues in the same video, 'are active atheists. They're like "in your face" atheist and they want to change policies and they're having debates. I don't have the time, the interest, the energy to do any of that.'[38] Now this seems a much more sensible claim than all the disingenuous stuff about not needing the word *atheist*. Here Tyson is clear to distinguish himself not from all atheists per se, but simply from what he calls 'active atheists'. These are the ones who really care about religion and actively oppose it, like Richard Dawkins. If Tyson is an atheist, he is like Mersault – he just doesn't really care about religion. And that, of course, is a perfectly respectable position.

6

Atheism and ethics

*Human decency is not derived
from religion. It precedes it.*

Christopher Hitchens[39]

Beliefs about right and wrong, and about how people should behave, have long been bound up with religion. Much of the Bible and the Koran are taken up with advice on what the faithful should and should not do. To many believers, morality comes from their god or gods, and they conclude that atheists must therefore lack any moral compass.

Most atheists reject this whole argument. Ethics can be based on non-religious foundations, they say, and it is therefore quite possible to be an atheist and still be a good person. Sure, it might be harder to figure out what is right and wrong if you can't simply go and look it up in a holy book, but might there not be value in this too – in the very fact that one must think carefully for oneself?

Moreover, the idea that moral laws are handed down from on high is not without difficulties of its own, as Socrates pointed out over 2,000 years ago. In Plato's dialogue *Euthyphro*, Socrates asks whether divine commandments are good simply because they are commanded by a god, or whether the god recognized what was good and pronounced his commandments accordingly. Socrates rejects the first option; if something is good only because a god commanded it, morality would be an arbitrary affair. Anything that a god happened to command would thereby become morally good! But if gods cannot be the source of ethical principles, we must seek such principles in the world independently of divine commandments. In other words, even a theist ends up a similar position to that of the atheist – having to use his or her reason to figure out what is good and bad. It won't be enough simply to know that a god commanded something – the true believer will want to know why their god commanded *this* rather than *that*.

And when one scrutinizes the various commandments and prohibitions that have supposedly been handed down by various gods, one finds some very curious things. Why, for example, should an all-powerful creator god be so adamant that his chosen people should refrain from eating pork, as Jews and Muslims claim? And why should people who commit adultery be put to death, as the Old Testament commands (Leviticus 20:10)? And why should cows be treated with such reverence, as some Hindus believe?

Four weird commandments

The Bible contains some very strange moral rules.

▶ It is forbidden to wear cloth made out of a mix of wool and linen, but other fibre combinations are fine. (Leviticus 19:19)

▶ Shaving is not allowed. Beards must be allowed to grow. (Leviticus 19:27)

▶ Do not touch women when they are having their period. (Leviticus 15:19–20)

▶ 'When men fight with one another, and the wife of the one draws near to rescue her husband from the hand of him who is beating him, and puts out her hand and seizes him by the private parts, then you shall cut off her hand.' (Deuteronomy 25:11–12)

These bizarre rules are hard to justify on any rational grounds; their apparent arbitrariness only makes sense in the light of their contingent historical origins. Perhaps the prohibition on pork arose out of public health concerns hundreds of years ago, at a time when pigs were indeed more likely to cause food poisoning or transmit diseases than other animals. Or perhaps these rules were deliberately arbitrary markers whose purpose was merely to identify believers and set them apart from non-believers. Whatever the precise historical explanation of these rules may be, their very contingency and parochialism detract from their pretensions to be universal moral laws and reveal them to be outdated human creations, unworthy of being respected today.

▶ What is good?

So how does an atheist begin to figure out if an action is good or bad? One way is to consider the consequences; an action is good if it increases the amount of happiness in the world, and bad if it reduces it. This approach is known as utilitarianism, and its most famous proponent was the philosopher Jeremy Bentham (1748–1832). According to Bentham, 'it is the greatest happiness of the greatest number that is the measure of right and wrong'.

For example, suppose someone asks you to donate money to a charity. Before you agree, you might consider the likely consequences of such an action. On the one hand, the small amount of money you have been asked to donate might buy a mosquito net or oral rehydration therapy that could save a child's life in Africa. But on the other hand, giving this money away means you won't be able to afford that book you were looking forward to reading.

How do you weigh these considerations against each other? You might reckon that the happiness achieved by saving a child's life will far outweigh the loss of your happiness caused by postponing your purchase of the book you want to read. In which case, you might feel obliged to donate the money to charity. But how can you be sure the charity will spend your donation appropriately? How much of your donation will go to paying the salary of charity workers, for example? And maybe there are already dozens of charities doing the same thing, with the result that there are mountains of unused mosquito nets lying around.

In fact, who says you even have a duty to increase the happiness of others? Utilitarianism holds that you should treat yourself with no essentially greater worth than anyone else, but this seems an impossibly high standard of behaviour. Furthermore, we know the desires and needs of others only imperfectly and we are not well situated to pursue them, while each of us is intimately familiar with our own individual wants and needs, and uniquely placed to pursue those wants and needs effectively. Therefore, if we set out to do good for others, it is likely that we will often bungle the job and end up doing more mischief than good. So perhaps the most moral thing to do is to attend always and only to our own wishes.

If moral arguments like this can end up going round and round in a circle without ever reaching a firm conclusion, then perhaps the best way to act is simply to consult one's moral intuitions. Decisions about right and wrong often evoke feelings, and these feelings can be a guide to how to act. The philosophers David Hume and Adam Smith championed this view, arguing that we had certain special 'moral sentiments' that provide us with a clear impression of wrongness when we see, for example, someone being mugged.

Where do these moral sentiments come from? Like most psychological traits, they are a mixture of nature and nurture. The social environment we grow up in will no doubt accentuate some values and downplay others. But there is a limit to what the social environment can do; there are no cultures anywhere, for example, where cheating your friends is held up as a moral act. The universal nature of many moral principles points to a biological origin for our moral sense, rooted in our shared evolutionary ancestry.

Research into the biological origins of morality is a relatively new field, but it is already beginning to yield some fascinating insights. Primatologists have found many analogues of moral behaviour in chimpanzees, and speculate that the common ancestor of humans and chimps may therefore have had complex moral emotions like inequality aversion and compassion. These findings reinforce the notion that we do not need divine guidance to develop moral systems; evolution has given us perfectly adequate moral feelings that may be a better basis for ethics than the writings of people who lived a few thousand years ago.

▶ Why be good?

Christians and Muslims believe that if they are good, their god will reward them by admitting them to heaven when they die, but that everlasting torment awaits them in hell if they are bad. This certainly seems like a powerful incentive to be good. But what about atheists? Why should they bother to be good if they think that there is no such thing as life after death?

This line of reasoning has led many believers to conclude that atheists must necessarily be less moral people than god-fearing folk. Yet it is worth pausing for a moment to consider what this says about the believers themselves. They are saying in effect that without the threat of hell to keep them in line and the promise of heaven to keep them sweet, they would probably be depraved sybarites, bloodthirsty murderers and unscrupulous cheats. If it is only the assurance of justice in the afterlife that keeps them from such heinous behaviour, they must surely be very vicious people at heart, and certainly not the kind of person one wishes to associate with.

To be honest, I doubt very much that most Christians or Muslims would plunge into a life of evil if they suddenly lost their faith. That is because, despite what they may say, their good behaviour is not based entirely on the fear of hell, nor on any of their religious beliefs, but on the same moral emotions that animate all of us, atheists included. Likewise, their bad behaviour, even when sanctioned by their religion, has psychological causes that have nothing to do with their faith. Bad people will always find excuses for doing bad things, whether religious or otherwise.

In any discussion of this topic, the atheist will sooner or later be confronted with the terrible crimes of Hitler, Stalin and Mao. These dictators were all atheists, the argument goes, and look what terrible things they did! But of course this proves nothing. Many bad things have been done in the name of religion too, such as the Crusades, the witch trials of the medieval and early modern periods and the terrorist attacks of 9/11. It is foolish to debate whether religious people or atheists have committed greater evils. The data do not seem very reliable, and it is not clear what would be gained even if we could find a reliable answer. Even if we discovered that, on balance, atheists were less moral than religious people, this would say nothing about whether gods exist or not. If the only way to make people behave morally is by getting them to believe in imaginary beings, it hardly seems a victory worth winning. Better to accept the brutal truth, and all the consequences that go with it, than to live in a permanent cloud cuckoo land.

Ultimately, atheists must find not just their own account of what it means to be good, but their own reasons for

How much harm does religion do?

'You don't get to advertise all the good that your religion does without first scrupulously subtracting all the harm it does and considering seriously the question of whether some other religion, or no religion at all, does better.'

Daniel Dennett, *Breaking the Spell: Religion as a Natural Phenomenon* (2007)

being good, if that is what they want to do. It may be that they enjoy striving to do the right thing for its own sake, or it may be that they do so for fear of social rejection. They may even decide that they don't care about being good at all. This is the kind of freedom that opens up to one who doesn't believe in gods, and who therefore has to accept the responsibility of confronting moral choices on one's own, without some imaginary friend holding one's hand.

▶ Breaking free of religious tradition

It would be rather surprising if, after lengthy consideration, a contemporary atheist were to come up with a moral code that was identical to that put forward by Christians. It would surely make one wonder whether the atheist had been sufficiently independent in his thinking, or whether he might not have been unconsciously influenced by the preceding centuries of Christian thought.

This possibility worried Friedrich Nietzsche. Writing at the end of the 19th century, he wondered whether atheists had gone far enough in freeing ethics from the religious trappings that had surrounded it for so long. Nietzsche argued that even as the influence of the Church declined in western Europe, the predominant moral values of most Europeans continued to be thoroughly Christian. Even those who no longer believed

▲ Friedrich Nietzsche (1844–1900), German philosopher, scholar and writer.

in a Christian god still subscribed to Christian values like pity, compassion, forgiveness and equality.

Nietzsche went on to develop what he called a 'genealogy of morals', tracing the origin of these Christian values to slaves in Ancient Greece and Rome. As such, these values reflected the slaves' conditions of existence. Of course slaves wanted equality, because that represented a step up from their condition of inferiority! Of course slaves wanted pity and forgiveness, rather than the violence that their masters inflicted on them! He contrasted this 'slave morality' with a different set of values that predominated among the aristocratic warrior class that owned the slaves. These values included courage, strength, nobility and an accurate sense of self-worth (rather than a false humility). At some point in history, the slaves had pulled off a brilliant trick; they had somehow fooled their masters into rejecting their original aristocratic values and adopting the value system of the slaves. This process began with the Jews, whose founding myth begins in slavery, and reached its culmination in the adoption of Christianity as the official religion of the Roman Empire.

Nietzsche on morality

'For believe me! – the secret for harvesting from existence the greatest fruitfulness and the greatest enjoyment is: to live dangerously! Build your cities on the slopes of Vesuvius! Send your ships into uncharted seas! Live at war with your peers and yourselves! Be robbers and conquerors as long as you cannot be rulers and possessors, you seekers of knowledge! Soon the age will be past when you could be content to live hidden in forests like shy deer! At long last the search for knowledge will reach out for its due: – it will want to rule and possess, and you with it!'

Friedrich Nietzsche, *The Gay Science: With a Prelude in Rhymes and an Appendix of Songs* (1882)

If we really wanted to purify ourselves of Christian influence, Nietzsche said, it was not enough to reject the Christian god; we should also purge ourselves of the slave morality that Christianity had injected like a virus into the bloodstream of western civilization. Hence atheists would do well, he argued, to reclaim the older aristocratic values that the Christians had all but eliminated. Atheists should not seek to be humble, compassionate and gentle, but courageous, noble and strong. They should not be afraid to seek their own glory and follow their own path wherever it led them, even if it meant trampling on the pathetic mediocrities that stood in their way.

The aristocratic values championed by Nietzsche may not be to everyone's taste, but they do at least provide an example of an alternative value system unencumbered by the residue of Christian thought, and they challenge atheists to come up with yet other value systems of their own devising. If we tremble at the thought of this, if the idea of breaking so radically with Christian tradition makes us afraid, then perhaps we are not as free of our Christian heritage as we like to believe. Perhaps the struggle to be truly ourselves, thoroughgoing atheists without the least residue of superstition clinging to our moral intuitions, is harder than we thought.

Atheism and ethics

7

Atheism and the meaning of life

Life has no meaning. Each of us has meaning and we bring it to life. It is a waste to be asking the question when you are the answer.

attributed to Joseph Campbell

The person who believes in gods finds himself in the midst of a great cosmic drama. All around him are spirits, angels, demons, vying for his attention and homage. Good and evil are locked in a cataclysmic struggle, and the believer is called upon to play his part. His life is imbued with transcendent meaning.

The atheist, by contrast, lives in a dead universe. The life that exists on this planet only emerged some nine billion years after the Big Bang, and will have vanished completely long before the Earth is swallowed up by the Sun seven billion years from now, as it swells into a red giant. Out there, in the rest of the galaxy, and in galaxies beyond our own, a few other life-bearing planets will suffer the same fate. And finally there will be nothing, as the universe continues to expand until it is too cold for anything to live.

Some atheists find this picture of the universe depressing, and wish there were some gods around to liven things up a bit. The physicist Steven Weinberg, for example, writes:

> 'It would be wonderful to find in the laws of nature a plan prepared by a concerned creator in which human beings played some special role. I find sadness in doubting that we will. There are some among my scientific colleagues who say that the contemplation of nature gives them all the spiritual satisfaction that others have traditionally found in a belief in an interested God. Some of them may even really feel that way. I do not.'[40]

Other atheists take a very different view, arguing that a godless universe has its own special kind of beauty; it simply requires a different aesthetic perspective to appreciate it. Charles Darwin attempted to evoke this godless kind of beauty in the final sentence of *On the Origin of Species*, in gorgeous prose:

> 'There is grandeur in this view of life, with its several powers, having been originally breathed into a few forms or into one; and that, whilst this planet has gone cycling on according to the fixed law of gravity, from so simple a beginning endless forms most beautiful and most wonderful have been, and are being, evolved.'[41]

Which of these perspectives one adopts is probably a matter of temperament. But it is not incumbent on the atheist to celebrate the fact that there are no gods; he is perfectly entitled to lament this state of affairs, and many have. Losing one's religion is a little like falling out of love. Being in love is a lot of fun, and it's sad when it fades. You don't have to pretend that it's wonderfully fulfilling to fall out of love to believe that you're better off accepting that it's the case.

However, even the most pessimistic atheist can recognize that religious pictures of the universe also have their downsides. It is not just that hell, for example, is a particularly frightening concept to contemplate; even heaven sounds rather unpleasant when you think about it. As the pop group Talking Heads sang: 'Heaven, heaven is a place, a place where nothing, nothing ever happens'. And as for the idea that there is someone who can look into your mind the whole time and know everything you are thinking, it is quite horrifying, and must constitute the ultimate paranoia.

There is also something refreshing and inspiring about having to find one's own meaning in life, rather than blindly accepting one prescribed in advance. If theism is like a prefabricated toy castle, atheism is more like a set of Lego blocks that offer the challenge and the opportunity of constructing one's own personal meaning of life, a meaning that is not put together according to any set of instructions handed down from on high.

The meaning of life

'There is something infantile in the presumption that somebody else (parents in the case of children, God in the case of adults) has a responsibility to give your life meaning and point ... The truly adult view, by contrast, is that our life is as meaningful, as full and as wonderful as we choose to make it.

'Richard Dawkins, *The God Delusion* (2006).

For atheists, their lives have no objective purpose; any purpose they have is a purely subjective one, a purpose they themselves have given to their lives. For some it may be to achieve happiness; for others it may be learn and grow wise; for yet others it may be to make the world a better place. This is certainly less grand than being created specifically for the purpose of worshipping god, or playing some other role in a vast cosmic drama. But it can be enough to make life worth living, and besides, a bit part in a cosmic drama is not to everyone's taste.

▶ Atheist spirituality?

A significant element of much religious practice throughout history has been the use of meditation, psychedelics and other means to induce altered states of consciousness. These so-called spiritual practices can be extremely rewarding and some atheists have wondered whether it might be possible to pursue them in a non-religious context. Could we, in other words, construct an atheist form of spirituality?

Some atheists baulk at the use of the word *spirituality* here, arguing that it has been irremediably tainted by its association with belief in gods. The prominent atheist philosopher Sam Harris disagrees. 'We must reclaim good words,' he argues, 'and put them to good use – and this is what I intend to do with 'spiritual' ... there seems to be no other term (apart from the even more problematic 'mystical' or the more restrictive 'contemplative') with which to discuss the deliberate efforts some people make to overcome their feeling of separateness – through meditation, psychedelics, or other means of inducing non-ordinary states of consciousness.'[42]

For Harris, then, it is quite legitimate to talk of atheist spirituality. After all, from an atheist perspective anyone who meditates or ingests a sacred weed is simply attempting to put their brain into a particular state in which certain thoughts and feelings become more available.

Science and spirituality

'Science is not only compatible with spirituality; it is a profound source of spirituality. When we recognize our place in an immensity of light-years and in the passage of ages, when we grasp the intricacy, beauty, and subtlety of life, then that soaring feeling, that sense of elation and humility combined, is surely spiritual. So are our emotions in the presence of great art or music or literature, or acts of exemplary selfless courage such as those of Mohandas Gandhi or Martin Luther King, Jr. The notion that science and spirituality are somehow mutually exclusive does a disservice to both.'

Carl Sagan, *The Demon-Haunted World: Science as a Candle in the Dark* (1997).

Believers and atheists may attribute these thoughts and feelings to different sources, but both may experience similar things, such as a sense of being at peace with the universe, or a greater love for their fellow human being.

The question of whether you can have spiritual atheists in a stronger sense is moot. Most atheists in the west hold a naturalistic world-view in which reality is exhaustively described by modern physics. There are many Buddhists in the east, though, who probably qualify as atheists, since they do not believe in any powerful supernatural beings who demand to be worshipped. These Buddhist atheists do not believe in the world described by modern physics, however. They believe that their souls will be reincarnated after they die, and that eventually they may escape the cycle of reincarnation when they attain enlightenment. This is clearly not a materialist world-view, but it is an atheist one. It is, in fact, an atheist religion.

Atheists are not necessarily materialists or physicalists, then, in the sense of believing that 'everything is physical' or that there is 'nothing over and above' the stuff described by modern physics. In practice, however, many atheists are in fact physicalists. Another name for this position is naturalism – the belief that only natural (as opposed to supernatural or spiritual) laws and forces operate in the world.

More recently, some have proposed a new name for those who subscribe to a naturalist world-view: 'brights'. This term was proposed by the writer Paul Geisert in 2003 as an umbrella term covering a range of narrower categories as atheists, agnostics, humanists and sceptics. Geisert disliked the label 'godless' and sought a new, positive word that might become widely accepted, in the same way that the term 'gay' has been embraced by the homosexual community. Personally, I find Geisert's proposal extremely obnoxious. Not all atheists want to be positive, warm and cheerful, and it is certainly not the case that atheists are necessarily any more intelligent than believers. For me, the term smacks of a narcissistic and arrogant self-regard. I prefer to keep things simple and call myself an atheist.

▶ An atheist church?

Humans are social animals and their search for meaning is rarely a solitary pursuit. Religions are predominantly social institutions, and provide believers with rich social networks for mutual support. Are atheists condemned to be outcasts, pursuing their own quest for meaning as isolated individuals? Or can they too construct social institutions of their own, non-religious organizations that can provide the same kind of succour as that which believers derive from their churches, mosques and ashrams? Is this even desirable?

Some atheists think so. Paul Geisert launched the Brights' Network in 2003 to provide a forum for atheists, sceptics and others with a naturalistic world-view to share their views and 'promote the civic understanding and acknowledgment of the naturalistic world-view'. Within a year, registered Brights numbered in five figures and spanned 85 nations. The movement has continued to grow ever since.

In 2013, two friends launched the Sunday Assembly in London as a weekly gathering for non-believers. Master of ceremonies Sanderson Jones calls it 'part foot-stomping show, part atheist church, all celebration of life'. On Sunday mornings a 'congregation' of more than 300 people crowds into a deconsecrated church to join the celebration. Instead of hymns, they sing along to Stevie Wonder and Queen songs. Few actively identify themselves as atheists. 'It's a nice excuse to get together and have a bit of a community spirit but without the religion aspect,' says one. Another suggests that people need a sense of connectedness in an increasingly atomized and individualistic society, and want to feel like they are 'part of something'.

▲ A Sunday Assembly meeting in London.

More prosaically, the past decade has seen the rapid growth of student atheist societies, sceptics' societies and other initiatives that provide avenues for atheists to meet each other and give each other support. In 2008, the National Federation of Atheist, Humanist and Secularist Student Societies was founded as an umbrella group bringing together the atheist, humanist and secular student societies in the UK and Republic of Ireland. They hold annual conventions, run campaigns, and raise money for charity.

These organizations may seem harmless, but to my mind there is something deeply suspicious about joining any group that defines itself in theological terms, whether theist or atheist. It is nice when like-minded people agree with you – too nice, in fact. Groups of people with similar beliefs rapidly become self-righteous cliques in which individual dissent is frowned upon. Religions have used the power of groupthink and social conformity to ensure their survival for centuries; by catering to our need to belong, they entice us into communities that make us feel warm and fuzzy, and thereby dull our critical faculties. 'Men, it has been well said, think in herds,' observed the writer Charles Mackay; 'it will be seen that they *go mad* in herds, while they only recover their senses slowly, and one by one'[43] (my italics). In my view, it is perverse for atheists to imitate the social aspects of religion. Hard though it may be, atheists should tread their paths alone.

Many atheists would probably disagree with this. They argue that discussion within groups of broad consensus can be valuable, since you can take certain assumptions for granted and focus on more complex questions. Members of a student atheist society might be able to debate with and learn from each other more effectively given that they start from an acknowledged common ground. So maybe it's possible to recognize the limitations of these groups and balance independent thought and collaboration, rather than striking out alone completely.

▶ The invisible friend

The believer, of course, is never alone. Even when there are no other people around, the believer always has a silent companion at his side, or so he imagines. You can occasionally see believers moving their lips silently, as if they are speaking to this imaginary friend, praying quietly to their gods. And they really believe that invisible beings are actually listening to them, even when they are just *thinking* their words!

It must be nice never to feel lonely, to believe that one or more powerful supernatural friends are constantly at your side, ready to comfort you whenever you need it. Atheists must live without that consolation. They will experience a kind of radical loneliness that true believers can never feel. Even when believers undergo a 'dark night of the soul', in which they feel abandoned by their gods, their faith tells them that god is still there, in the background. Atheists know that there are no gods anywhere, not even lurking in the distance, and that as a result they are completely and utterly alone.

Atheism and antitheism

'I am not even an atheist so much as I am an antitheist; I not only maintain that all religions are versions of the same untruth, but I hold that the influence of churches, and the effect of religious belief, is positively harmful. Reviewing the false claims of religion I do not wish, as some sentimental materialists affect to wish, that they were true. I do not envy believers their faith. I am relieved to think that the whole story is a sinister fairy tale; life would be miserable if what the faithful affirmed was actually the case [....] there may be people who wish to live their lives under a cradle-to-grave divine supervision; a permanent surveillance and monitoring. But I cannot imagine anything more horrible or grotesque.'

Christopher Hitchens, *Letters to a Young Contrarian* (2001)

Yet to my mind this radical loneliness offers far greater opportunities for personal development than any imaginary friend could possibly provide. It is normal for children to feel lost without their parents, but one of the challenges of growing up is learning to do without them and standing on one's own two feet. Psychological maturity involves taking responsibility for one's own life; handing over responsibility to a guru, a cult leader or an imaginary friend is a cop-out, an act of cowardice, and refusal to grow up. No man is an island, but each one of us must ultimately decide his own fate, and each one of us must ultimately die alone. The courage to confront this ultimate solitude is one of the greatest virtues, and only atheists can truly acquire it.

It is worth emphasizing that this is a personal position, and that my individualistic approach isn't integral to atheism. An atheist with a more communitarian leaning would probably take a different view.

▶ Life after death

Humans are the only animals that are conscious of their mortality. We are the only creatures who can torture ourselves with the thought that, one day, we will no longer think or feel or laugh or cry. When a child first becomes conscious of this and tries to wrap his or her mind around the unthinkable notion of ceasing to exist, of plunging into eternal oblivion, it is a dreadful moment. This is the beginning of the end of childhood; the shadow of death will haunt the person for the rest of his or her life. What will it be like, not to exist any more? How brief life is, compared with the eternity of non-existence that follows it. How awful, for this wonderful bright spark of being that is me, for this precious self-consciousness, to disappear forever.

And how comforting, therefore, to think that death is not the end – that it is merely a transition to some other form of existence, either in heaven or reincarnated as another human, or even as a different species. One of the most powerful attractions of religion is no doubt the promise of eternal life. Belief in gods has always been accompanied by a belief in life after death. Humans are unlike other animals in that they bury their dead, and this is often accompanied by religious rituals. Human skeletal remains dating back 100,000 years have been discovered in Israel and were accompanied by a variety of grave goods. Such intentional burial, with the grave goods probably intended for the afterlife, may be one of the earliest detectable forms of religious practice. Even today, most funerals are conducted according to Christian, Muslim, Jewish or Hindu prescriptions, and prayers are offered for the dead.

But what point is there in such consolations if they are mere fictions? It matters little how nice it would be to believe in something, if that something is not true. The atheist must confront the reality of death without the aid of comforting fairy tales. He must look death in the face, and make his own peace with it. But once again, this austere discipline offers a far greater opportunity for personal growth than any promises of eternal life could possibly provide. Only someone who has come to terms with the certainty of his own eventual extinction, his complete and total annihilation, can truly be said to have attained psychological maturity. And such maturity is, therefore, forever denied to the believer. Theists are condemned to remain forever children.

There is a tragic beauty in the transience of human existence. Like the cherry trees that blossom so brilliantly yet so briefly, life's brevity is itself an essential part of its loveliness. Atheists can love life *because* it is short and finite – without any misguided grasping after illusory permanence. They are less likely to waste their lives when they know that this is the only one they have. They can decide to live every moment to the full, with an intensity that is only possible to those who know their time is limited. As the critic Walter Pater wrote:

> 'A counted number of pulses only is given to us of a variegated, dramatic life. How may we see in them all that is to be seen in them by the finest senses? How shall we pass most swiftly from point to point, and be present always at the focus where the greatest number of vital forces unite in their purest energy? ... With this sense of the splendour of our experience and of its awful brevity, gathering all we are into one desperate effort to see and touch, we shall hardly have time to make theories about the things we see and touch.'[44]

There are some atheists, nevertheless, who still want to live forever, and believe that they may achieve by scientific means what religion has vainly promised to the faithful. Several hundred people have already undergone cryopreservation procedures, which involve cooling the body as soon as a person has died, in the hope that resuscitation may be possible in the future with advanced technology able to preserve human life indefinitely. Perhaps they will even upload their consciousness into artificial brains in robotic bodies and live for millions of years. Eventually, though, even they will die, when the universe becomes so cold that it cannot sustain any life, whether of the natural or artificial kind.

But even if they could find a way of surviving the heat death of the universe and literally live forever, what would these atheists be living *for*? Presumably, they must know that now, or they wouldn't want to stay alive forever. They must know what makes life worth living *right now*, in other words. And if they know that, then does it really matter whether they live another 10 years, or another thousand? Once you know what makes your life worth living *today*, what it is that gets you out of bed each morning, then you acquire a peace of mind that dispels any fear of death. One is ready, as it were, to die at any moment – to die right now, even – because one is fully and completely alive, and has not kept anything back. If, on the other hand, you don't know why you bother to keep struggling, you don't know what you are living for, then you could live another thousand years like that and still die unhappy and full of regrets. This is why Albert Camus stated that the only truly serious philosophical problem is suicide. 'Judging whether life is or is not worth living,' he wrote, 'amounts to answering the fundamental question of philosophy. All the rest – whether or not the world has three dimensions, whether the mind has nine or twelve categories – comes afterwards. These are games; one must first answer.'[45]

Each atheist must find his or her own answer to this question, but I find Pater's emphasis on living in the moment and experiencing life to the full to be a key part of my own response. I will, therefore, leave the closing lines of this book to him:

> 'We are all condamnés, as Victor Hugo says: we are all under sentence of death, but with a sort of indefinite reprieve – les hommes sont tous condamnés à mort avec des sursis indéfinis: we have an interval, and then our place knows no more. Some spend this interval in listlessness, some in high passion, the wisest, at least among "the children of the world", in art and song. For our one chance lies in expanding that interval, in getting as many pulsations as possible into the given time.'[46]

Penn Jillette's ten commandments for atheists

1 The highest ideals are human intelligence, creativity and love. Respect these above all.

2 Do not put things or even ideas above other human beings.

3 Say what you mean, even when talking to yourself.

4 Put aside some time to rest and think.

5 Be there for your family. Love your parents, your partner and your children.

6 Respect and protect all human life.

7 Keep your promises.

8 Don't steal.

9 Don't lie.

10 Don't waste too much time wishing, hoping and being envious; it'll make you bugnutty.

Five top websites

11 https://humanism.org.uk Founded in 1896, the British Humanist Association (BHA) is a British charity working on behalf of non-religious people who seek to live ethical and fulfilling lives on the basis of reason and humanity. It has over 28,000 members and supporters. It also trains celebrants to conduct humanist funerals and weddings and other non-religious ceremonies.

12 **www.atheists.org** Founded in 1963, American Atheists fights for the civil liberties of atheists and the total and absolute separation of government and religion. American Atheists was born out of a court case begun in 1959 by the Murray family that challenged prayer recitation in public-sector schools.

13 **www.the-brights.net** Launched in 2003 by Paul Geisert, the Brights' Network provides a forum for atheists, sceptics and others with a naturalistic worldview to share their views and 'promote the civic understanding and acknowledgment of the naturalistic worldview'.

14 **http://atheistscholar.org** The Atheist Scholar is an online academic resource for those interested in the serious, interdisciplinary study of atheism. The website provides a comprehensive overview for the student of atheism, a review of the best books on atheism, and summaries of literature and movies of interest to atheists.

15 **www.atheistalliance.org** Atheist Alliance International (AAI) is a global federation of atheist and free-thought groups and individuals, committed to educating its members and the public about atheism, secularism and related issues. AAI aims to challenge and confront religious faith and promote the growth and interaction of atheist/free-thought organizations around the world.

Five top blogs

16 **http://scienceblogs.com/pharyngula/** Pharyngula is a blog written by the biologist and famous atheist PZ Myers. In 2006, the science journal *Nature* listed it as the top-ranked blog written by a scientist. It has become particularly well-known for Myers' writing style (characterized by sarcasm) and criticism of intelligent design and creationism. In 2009, Pharyngula was ranked the most popular atheist blog.

17 www.patheos.com/blogs/friendlyatheist/ The Friendly Atheist blog is written by Hemant Mehta, who is also a regular speaker at free-thought and sceptical events around the USA. The blog attempts to build bridges of understanding between believers and non-believers.

18 http://dwindlinginunbelief.blogspot.com On the Dwindling in Unbelief blog, Steve Wells, author of the amazing *Skeptic's Annotated Bible*, offers acute sceptical analysis of the Bible.

19 http://debunkingchristianity.blogspot.com Debunking Christianity is the blog of atheist author John Loftus, a former Christian apologist.

20 www.atheistmedia.com Atheist Media Blog is an excellent daily source of news and videos on science and religion.

Ten famous contemporary atheists

21 Richard Dawkins (1941–), British ethologist, evolutionary biologist and writer. Dawkins is without doubt the most famous atheist alive today. Together with Hitchens, Dennett and Harris, he has promoted an outspoken approach that has been dubbed 'the New Atheism'.

22 Christopher Hitchens (1949–2011), British-American journalist and author. In essays, books and public debates Hitchens proved to be the most eloquent and most biting of the so-called 'New Atheists'. Before he died from cancer in 2011, he dismissed the notion of a possible deathbed conversion, noting that 'redemption and supernatural

deliverance appears even more hollow and artificial to me than it did before'.

23 **Daniel Dennett** (1942–), American philosopher, author and cognitive scientist. Dennett is the world's greatest living philosopher. His books on Darwinism, cognitive science and religion all combine great depth with extreme lucidity. His approach tends to be more calm and sober than that of Dawkins and Hitchens.

24 **Sam Harris** (1967–), American author, philosopher and neuroscientist. Harris' 2004 book *The End of Faith* was on the *New York Times* bestseller list for 33 weeks and was followed in 2006 by *Letter to a Christian Nation*. Unlike the other 'New Atheists', Harris actively seeks to incorporate spirituality in the domain of human reason. He draws inspiration from the practices of Eastern religion, in particular that of meditation.

25 **Alain de Botton** (1969–), Anglo-Swiss philosopher, author and documentary maker. De Botton takes a much more positive view of religion than the 'New Atheists', and believes that atheists can salvage valuable elements from the religions whose beliefs they discard.

26 **Paul 'PZ' Myers** (1957–), American evolutionary developmental scientist. PZ is the author of Pharyngula, one of the top-ranked science blogs. He is known for his wit and sarcasm, and for his trenchant criticism of intelligent design and creationism.

27 **Ayaan Hirsi Ali** (1969–), Somali-born activist, writer and politician. Hirsi identified as Muslim until 2002, when she announced that after a long intellectual journey she was now an atheist. When she collaborated with the Dutch film director Theo van Gogh on a short movie critical of Islam, they both received death threats, and van Gogh was later assassinated by a Dutch Muslim.

28 Steven Pinker (1954–), Canadian experimental psychologist, cognitive scientist and author. Pinker was named one of *Time* magazine's 100 most influential scientists and thinkers in the world in 2004 and has received numerous similar accolades. His books on cognitive science and evolutionary psychology are intellectual blockbusters, always characterized by careful and incisive analysis.

29 Douglas Adams (1952–2001), British writer and dramatist. The author of *The Hitchhiker's Guide to the Galaxy*, Adams was a brilliant humorist and dramatist, and he often put his wit to devastating effect when mocking religion. Adams described himself as a 'radical atheist', adding the word 'radical' for emphasis so he would not be asked if he meant 'agnostic'.

30 Noam Chomsky (1928–), American linguist, philosopher and cognitive scientist. When asked if he was an atheist, Chomsky replied 'What is it that I'm supposed to not believe in? Until you can answer that question I can't tell you whether I'm an atheist.' Only an atheist would reply like that.

Ten atheist celebrities

31 Angelina Jolie (1975–), American actress and film director. 'There doesn't need to be a God for me. There's something in people that's spiritual, that's godlike. I don't feel like doing things just because people say things, but I also don't really know if it's better to just not believe in anything, either.'

32 Warren Buffet (1930–), American businessman, investment guru and philanthropist. According to Roger Lowenstein in *Buffett: The Making of an American Capitalist* (Doubleday, 1995; page 13), even at a young age, Buffett was too mathematical and too logical to subscribe to his family's religious beliefs. 'He adopted his father's ethical underpinnings, but not his belief in an unseen divinity.'

33 **Jodie Foster** (1962–), American actress, film director and producer. 'I'm an atheist. But I absolutely love religions and the rituals. Even though I don't believe in God. We celebrate pretty much every religion in our family with the kids. They love it, and when they say, "Are we Jewish?" or "Are we Catholic?" I say, "Well, I'm not, but you can choose when you're 18."'

34 **Björk** (1965–), Icelandic singer-songwriter, music producer and actress. 'I've got my own religion. Iceland sets a world-record. The UN asked people from all over the world a series of questions. Iceland stuck out on one thing. When we were asked what we believe, 90 per cent said, "ourselves". I think I'm in that group. If I get into trouble, there's no God or Allah to sort me out. I have to do it myself.'

35 **Ricky Gervais** (1961–), British comedian, actor and writer. 'I've never been insulted by hateful satanists for not believing in their devil. Only by loving Christians for not believing in their God.'

36 **Stephen Fry** (1957–), British comedian, actor, writer and presenter. 'I've always believed that everything said from authority is either the authority of one's own heart, one's own brain, one's own reading, one's own trust, but not the authority of someone who claims it because they're speaking for God and they know the truth because it's written in a book. That, essentially, is where I come from. In a sense, tolerance is my religion. Reason is my religion.'

37 **Daniel Radcliffe** (1989–), British actor. 'I'm an atheist, but I'm very relaxed about it. I don't preach my atheism, but I have a huge amount of respect for people like Richard Dawkins who do.'

38 Bill Gates (1955–), American computer scientist, businessman and philanthropist. 'Just in terms of allocation of time resources, religion is not very efficient. There's a lot more I could be doing on a Sunday morning.'

39 Kiera Knightley (1985–), British film actress. 'If only I wasn't an atheist; I could get away with anything. You'd just ask for forgiveness, and then you'd be forgiven.'

40 Brad Pitt (1963–), American actor and film producer 'I'm probably 20 per cent atheist and 80 per cent agnostic. I don't think anyone really knows. You'll either find out or not when you get there, until then there's no point thinking about it.'

Ten non-fiction books

41 Julien Offray de La Mettrie, *L'Homme machine* (1748). Variously translated as 'Man, a Machine' or 'Machine Man', this work of materialist philosophy extended Descartes' argument that animals are mere automatons or machines to human beings, denying the existence of the soul as a substance separate from matter. Even the relatively tolerant Dutch were scandalized, forcing La Mettrie to flee to Prussia.

42 Charles Darwin, *On the Origin of Species* (1859). In this seminal work, Darwin lays out his theory of natural selection in lucid and compelling prose. By describing a purely physical mechanism by which complex design can emerge without the assistance of any intelligent designer, Darwin showed that animals and plants need not be the work of a creator god.

43 Bertrand Russell, *Why I Am Not a Christian* (1927). This 1927 essay by the British philosopher Bertrand Russell is a brilliant and concise refutation of arguments for the existence of God. Russell also casts doubt on the historical existence of Jesus and questions the morality of religion: 'I say quite deliberately that the Christian religion, as organized in its churches, has been and still is the principal enemy of moral progress in the world.'

44 Carl Sagan, *The Demon-Haunted World: Science as a Candle in the Dark* (1996). In this masterpiece of popular science writing, the astrophysicist Carl Sagan describes the scientific method and presents a set of tools for sceptical thinking, which he calls a 'baloney detection kit'.

45 Sam Harris, *The End of Faith: Religion, Terror, and the Future of Reason* (2003). Like other 'New Atheists', Harris was profoundly affected by the attacks of 11 September 2001 in the USA. He wrote this book as a response, and the result is a powerful criticism of all styles of religious belief, both extremist and moderate.

46 Richard Dawkins, *The God Delusion* (2006). Dawkins' atheist blockbuster offers a lucid and devastating criticism of belief in gods, and has provoked widespread commentary. Dawkins also attacks the teaching of religion in schools, calling it a form of mental abuse.

47 Daniel Dennett, *Breaking the Spell: Religion as a Natural Phenomenon* (2006). Dennett provides an accessible and balanced overview of the latest scientific theories about the origins of religious belief.

48 Christopher Hitchens, *God is Not Great: How Religion Poisons Everything* (2007). In this exquisitely written diatribe, Hitchens excoriates religious belief, especially of the Christian and Muslim kind, in what is perhaps the most powerful statement of atheism in recent times.

49 Victor J. Stenger, *God: The Failed Hypothesis* (2007). This *New York Times* bestseller argues that there is no evidence for the existence of a deity and concludes that the existence of gods, while not impossible, is improbable. Drawing from cosmology, particle physics and quantum mechanics, Stenger shows that the universe is best explained as a purely natural phenomenon.

50 Penn Jillette, *God, No! Signs You May Already Be an Atheist and Other Magical Tales* (2011). As one might expect from the illusionist and comedian Penn Jillette, this book is much more light-hearted in tone than those above. Described as an atheist bible of sorts by reviewers, the book includes an atheist's take on the 10 commandments (see numbers 1–10 in this section).

Five works of fiction

51 Voltaire, *Candide, ou l'Optimisme (Candide, or Optimism)* (1759). This famous satire tells the story of a young man, Candide, and his loss of faith in the optimistic creed that 'all is for the best in this best of all possible worlds'. Voltaire's real target was the German philosopher Leibniz, who tried to justify the imperfections of the world by claiming that this must be the best possible and most balanced world, because it was created by an all-powerful and all-knowing God.

52 Marquis de Sade, *Dialogue entre un prêtre et un moribond* (*Dialogue between a priest and a dying man*) (1782). In this deliciously twisted tale by the wonderfully wicked Marquis de Sade, a priest comes to a dying atheist to give him the last rites, but instead of meekly confessing his sins, the atheist uses his final moments to destroy the priest's faith.

53 Friedrich Nietzsche, *Also sprach Zarathustra (Thus Spake Zarathustra)* (1883–5). This extended parable tells the story of Zarathustra, a kind of atheist prophet, who decides to share his hard-earned wisdom with others.

Much of it is obscure and cryptic, but it also contains some powerful passages, including the parable on the 'death of God'. Not for the faint-hearted!

54 **Albert Camus, *L'Étranger (The Outsider)* (1942).** This famous novel by the philosopher Albert Camus tells the story of Meursault, an Algerian man who kills an Arab for no apparent reason. Meursault is an atheist, though a rather indifferent one. What makes him especially appealing to atheists is not, however, his lack of belief in gods, but his refusal to play by the rules of conventional society.

55 **Philip Pullman, *His Dark Materials* trilogy: *Northern Lights*** (published as *The Golden Compass* in North America), *The Subtle Knife*, *The Amber Spyglass* (1995–2000). The books in the *His Dark Materials* trilogy have been attacked by Christians for their scathing attitude to religion, especially Roman Catholicism. Others have viewed the series as an atheist alternative to C S Lewis's Narnia Chronicles, which Pullman has criticized as religious propaganda.

Ten top quotations

56 'We are all atheists about most of the gods that humanity has ever believed in. Some of us just go one god further.' Richard Dawkins.

57 'Isn't it enough to see that a garden is beautiful without having to believe that there are fairies at the bottom of it too?' Douglas Adams.

58 'The Bible has noble poetry in it ... and some good morals and a wealth of obscenity, and upwards of a thousand lies.' Mark Twain.

59 'Isn't that [an agnostic] just an atheist without balls?' Stephen Colbert.

60 'Properly read, the Bible is the most potent force for atheism ever conceived.' Isaac Asimov.

61 'With or without religion, you would have good people doing good things and evil people doing evil things. But for good people to do evil things, that takes religion.' Steven Weinberg.

62 'She believed in nothing. Only her scepticism kept her from being an atheist.' Jean-Paul Sartre.

63 'The reason people use a crucifix against vampires is because vampires are allergic to bullshit.' Richard Pryor.

64 'Eternal suffering awaits anyone who questions god's infinite love.' Bill Hicks.

65 'There was a time when religion ruled the world. It is known as the Dark Ages.' Ruth Hurmence Green.

Five jokes

66 'When I told the people of Northern Ireland that I was an atheist, a woman in the audience stood up and said, "Yes, but is the God of the Catholics or the God of the Protestants in whom you don't believe?"' Quentin Crisp (1908–99), British writer and raconteur.

67 You know when you close your eyes and really wish hard for something? Well, God's the guy who ignores you.

68 I was at church the other day and when the collection came around I put some Monopoly money in the basket. The priest said to me, 'What are you doing? That's not real money!' I replied, 'Well, let's talk about this god of yours …'

69 Did you know, if you rearrange the letters in 'religion' it spells 'ngoiilre'? Yeah, still makes absolutely no sense.

70 Blasphemy is a victimless crime.

Five movies

71 *Monty Python's Life of Brian* (1979), a comedy set in Roman-ruled Palestine around 30 CE; director, Terry Jones. This hilarious satire on the life of Jesus tells the story of Brian Cohen, a young Jewish man who is born on the same day as, and next door to, Jesus Christ, and is subsequently mistaken for the Messiah. Some countries, including Ireland and Norway, banned it when it came out, with a few of these bans lasting decades.

72 *Religulous* (2008), a documentary with Bill Maher; director, Larry Charles. Comedian Bill Maher travels to numerous religious destinations, including Jerusalem, the Vatican and Salt Lake City, interviewing believers from a variety of backgrounds and groups, and generally making fun of them.

73 *Agora* (2009), a historical drama starring Rachel Weisz, Max Minghella and Oscar Isaac; director, Alejandro Amenábar. This fascinating historical drama tells the story of Hypatia, a female mathematician, philosopher and astronomer in fourth-century Roman Egypt, who struggles to save the knowledge of classical antiquity from destruction. Set against the background of the rise of Christianity, it explores the fraught relationship between science and religion.

74 *The Invention of Lying* (2009), a comedy starring Ricky Gervais, Jennifer Garner and Jonah Hill; directors, Ricky Gervais, Matthew Robinson. This romantic comedy stars Ricky Gervais as Mark Bellison, the first human with the ability to lie. When his mother has a heart attack, Mark tells her that she will go to heaven, and she dies happily. Mark builds on his lie to create a new religion, telling everyone that he talks to a 'Man in the Sky' who controls everything and promises great rewards in the good place after you die, as long as you do no more than three bad things.

75 *The Ledge* (2011), a drama starring Charlie Hunnam, Terrence Howard and Patrick Wilson; director, Matthew Chapman. A complex love triangle develops between an atheist, a fundamentalist Christian and the woman they both love. The atheist and the Christian despise each other, but their philosophical differences turn out to be placeholders for deeper emotional issues.

Five songs

76 'Imagine' by John Lennon; released 1971.

77 'God's Song' by Randy Newman, on the 'Sail Away' album; released 1972.

78 'The Pope Song' by Tim Minchin; released 2010.

79 'Leper Messiah' by Metallica, on the 'Master of Puppets' album; released 1986.

80 'Losing My Religion' by R.E.M., on the 'Out of Time' album; released 1991.

Five common misconceptions about atheists

81 Atheists feel that their lives are meaningless.

82 Atheists have no motivation to be good, since they do not believe in heaven or hell.

83 Atheists are intolerant, and prejudiced against religious people.

84 Atheists cannot be patriotic or good citizens.

85 Atheists are more rational than religious believers.

Five questions that atheists should ask believers

86 If your god is all-powerful and all-loving, why is there so much suffering in the world?

87 Why are there so many contradictions in your holy book?

88 Why is your god so desperate for you to worship him?

89 If your god is so clever, why did he design humans so badly?

90 If your god is so loving, why does he send people to hell?

Five religious festivals that atheists should see

91 **Kumbha Mela**, India. The Kumbh Mela is a mass pilgrimage in which Hindus gather to bathe in the sacred river Ganges. It is considered to be the largest peaceful gathering in the world, with over 100 million people present in 2013. It is held every third year at one of four locations by rotation: Haridwar, Allahabad (Prayaga), Nashik and Ujjain.

92 **Holy Week**, Seville, Spain, or Antigua, Guatemala. The Roman Catholic penitential processions during Holy Week (the week before Easter) in Seville and Antigua are famous for the huge statues of Jesus and the Virgin Mary borne aloft by teams of penitents dressed in flowing robes. In Antigua, the streets are adorned with colourful 'carpets' made from coloured sawdust, flowers, fruit and vegetables.

93 **Inti Raymi** (24 June), Cuzco, Peru. A reconstruction of the Inca festival of the Sun. In the Inca Empire, the Inti Raymi was the most important ceremony celebrated in the capital city, Cuzco, and it is still celebrated today by indigenous peoples throughout the Andes. The celebrations involve music, colourful costumes and the sharing of food.

94 The Day of the Dead (31 October–2 November), Mexico. This Mexican holiday focuses on gatherings of family and friends to pray for and remember those who have died. Traditions connected with the holiday include building private altars called *ofrendas*, honouring the deceased using sugar skulls, marigolds and the favourite foods and beverages of the departed, and visiting graves with these as gifts. The festival retains many traces of its Aztec origins.

95 Tết, Vietnam. Tết is the Vietnamese New Year, and is the most important celebration of Vietnamese culture. The customs practised during Tết include visiting a person's house on the first day of the New Year, ancestor worship, wishing people a happy New Year, and giving lucky money to children and elderly people.

Five religious texts that atheists should read

96 The Bible. The Christian holy book is divided into two parts: the Old Testament, which contains the 24 books of the Hebrew Bible divided into 39 books and ordered differently from the Hebrew Bible; and the New Testament, which tells the story of Jesus and the early Christian church. The Old Testament was largely compiled between the sixth and fourth centuries BCE, while the New Testament was composed in the first two centuries CE.

97 The Koran. The Muslim holy book was pieced together during the seventh century CE from fragments that supposedly record the sayings of Muhammad. Muslims believe that the words were dictated to Muhammad by an angel, but if so the angel seems to have been something of a plagiarist, since most of the contents are poorly retold versions of pre-existing Jewish, Christian and Arab traditions.

98 The Popol Vuh. The Popol Vuh recounts some important Maya myths, including the origin of humanity and the epic tales of the Hero Twins, Hunahpú and Xbalanqué. It offers a fascinating glimpse into the pre-Columbian religions of Central America.

99 The Rig Veda. The Rig Veda. is a collection of Vedic Sanskrit hymns that are still recited as Hindu prayers at religious functions. It is one of the four canonical sacred texts (*śruti*) of Hinduism known as the Vedas. Composed between *c.* 1500–1200 BCE, it contains several mythological accounts of the origin of the world, hymns praising the gods, and ancient prayers for life and prosperity.

100 The Prose Edda. This is an Old Norse compilation of pagan Scandinavian mythology made in Iceland in the early 13th century. Replete with giants, elves, wolves and serpents, this is Tolkein on steroids!

Notes

Chapter 1

1 Stephen Colbert to Bart Ehrman on his TV comedy show *The Colbert Report*, 20 June 2006.

2 Jonathan Miller in his 2004 BBC TV documentary series *Atheism: A Rough History of Disbelief* (screened in US as *A Brief History of Disbelief*).

3 Neil deGrasse Tyson at www.youtube.com/watch?v=CzSMC5rWvos (accessed 23 June 2014).

4 Daniel Dennett at http://meaningoflife.tv/transcript.php?speaker=dennett (accessed 23 June 2014).

5 J. J. C. Smart, 'Atheism and Agnosticism', in Edward N. Zalta (ed.) *The Stanford Encyclopedia of Philosophy* (spring 2013), at http://plato.stanford.edu/archives/spr2013/entries/atheism-agnosticism/ (accessed 23 June 2014).

Chapter 2

6 Steven Weinberg, *Dreams of a Final Theory: The Scientist's Search for the Ultimate Laws of Nature* (New York: Pantheon Books, 1992), p. 256.

7 Albert Einstein, upon being asked if he believed in God by Rabbi Herbert Goldstein of the Institutional Synagogue, New York, 24 April 1921, published in the *New York Times*, 25 April 1929; from Ronald W. Clark, *Einstein: The Life and Times* (New York: World Publishing Co., 1971), p. 413. Also cited as a telegram to a Jewish newspaper, 1929, Einstein Archive 33-272, from Alice Calaprice (ed.), *The Expanded Quotable Einstein* (Princeton, NJ: Princeton University Press, 2000), p. 204.

8 Richard Dawkins, *A Devil's Chaplain: Selected Essays* (London: Weidenfeld & Nicolson, 2003), p. 150.

9 Robert Jay Lifton, *Thought Reform and the Psychology of Totalism: A Study of 'Brainwashing' in China* (New York: W. W. Norton, 1961), p. 434.

10 Ibid, p. 434.

11 Ibid, p. 434.

12 Miron Zuckerman, Jordan Silberman and Judith A. Hall, 'The Relation Between Intelligence and Religiosity: A Meta-Analysis and Some Proposed Explanations', *Personality and Social Psychology Review*, 6 August 2013; doi: 10.1177/1088868313497266 (accessed 23 June 2014).

13 William of Ockham, *Summa Logicae* (c.1323), cited in Dale T. Irvin and Scott W. Sunquist, *History of the World Christian Movement*, Volume I: Earliest Christianity to 1453, p. 434.

14 Søren Kierkegaard, *Concluding Unscientific Postscript to Philosophical Fragments*, Volume 1 (Kierkegaard's Writings, Vol. 12.1), ed. and trans. Howard V. Hong and Edna H. Hong, (Princeton: Princeton University Press, 1992), p.335.

15 William Paley, *Natural Theology or Evidences of the Existence and Attributes of the Deity* (London: J. Faulder, 14th edn, 1813), p. 1.

Chapter 3

16 Quoted in Annie Laure Gaylor, *Women Without Superstition* (Madiscon, WI: Freedom From Religion Foundation, 1997), pp. 469–85.

17 Paul Henri Thiry, Baron d'Holbach, *Système de la Nature ou Des Loix du Monde Physique et du Monde Moral* (*The System of Nature or, The Laws of the Moral and Physical World*) (1770), p.49; at www.amazon.co.uk/System-Nature-1-Baron-DHolbach-ebook/dp/B0082RZL9S (accessed 23 June 2014).

18 Karl Marx, introduction to the proposed but unwritten 'A Contribution to the Critique of Hegel's Philosophy of Right'; the introduction (written 1843) was published in Marx's journal *Deutsch-Französische Jahrbücher* in 1844.

19 http://en.wikipedia.org/wiki/Jesus (accessed 23 June 2014).

20 http://en.wikipedia.org/wiki/Muhammad (accessed 23 June 2014).

21 Max Weber in a lecture, 'Wissenschaft als Beruf' ('Science as a Vocation'), given in 1917 at Munich University; at http://en.wikipedia.org/wiki/Science_as_a_Vocation (accessed 23 June 2014).

Chapter 4

22 Kurt Vonnegut, *Palm Sunday: An Autobiographical Collage* (New York: Dial Press, 2011), p. 196.

23 B. F. Skinner, '"Superstition" in the Pigeon', *Journal of Experimental Psychology*, Vol. 38, 1948, p. 168.

24 Ibid.

25 Justin Barrett, 'Exploring the natural foundations of religion', *Trends in Cognitive Sciences*, Vol. 4, No. 1, January 2000, p. 31.

26 Daniel Dennett, *Breaking the Spell: Religion as a Natural Phenomenon* (London: Penguin, 2007), p. 17.

27 Ibid, pp. 17–18.

28 Richard Dawkins in the 'God on the Brain' episode of the BBC TV *Horizon* documentary series, broadcast 17 April 2003.

29 Nicholas Humphrey, *Leaps of Faith: Science, Miracles, and the Search for Supernatural Consolation* (New York: Basic Books, 1996), p. 99.

Chapter 5

30 Marquis de Sade, *Justine, Philosophy in the Bedroom, and Other Writings*, ed. and trans. Richard Seaver and Austryn Wainhouse (New York: Grove Press, 1990) p. 174.

31 Frank Furedi, 'The curious rise of anti-religious hysteria' (23 January 2006), at www.spiked-online.com/newsite/article/128#.U49thXaiXaI (accessed 23 June 2014).

32 David Hume, 'Of the standard of taste' (1757), at http://www.csulb.edu/~jvancamp/361r15.html (accessed 23 June 2014)

33 Ibid.

34 Ibid.

35 Ibid.

36 Nicholas Humphrey, 'What shall we tell the children?' (Oxford Amnesty lecture 1997), *The Mind Made Flesh: Frontiers of Psychology and Evolution* (Oxford: Oxford University Press, 2002), p. 291.

37 Albert Camus, *The Outsider*, trans. Joseph Laredo, (London: Penguin, 2000), p. 111.

38 Tyson, op. cit.

Chapter 6

39 Christopher Hitchens, *God is Not Great: How Religion Poisons Everything* (New York: Warner Twelve, 2007), p. 266.

Chapter 7

40 Weinberg, op. cit., p. 256.

41 Charles Darwin, *On the Origin of Species* (1859), (Oxford: Oxford University Press, 2008), p. 360.

42 Sam Harris, 'In defense of "spiritual"' (27 June 2012), at www.samharris.org/blog/item/a-plea-for-spirituality (accessed 23 June 2014).

43 Charles Mackay, *Memoirs of Extraordinary Popular Delusions and the Madness of Crowds* (1852), at www.gutenberg.org/files/24518/24518-h/dvi.html#preface (accessed 23 June 2014)

44 Walter Pater, *The Renaissance* (1873), (New York: Cosimo, 2005) p. 197.

45 Albert Camus, 'The Myth of Sisyphus', *The Myth of Sisyphus and Other Essays*, trans. Justin O'Brien (New York: Vintage, 1991), p. 3.

46 Walter Pater, op. cit., p.198.

Picture credits

The author and publisher would like to give their thanks for permission to use the following images:

Pussy Riot protest, Moscow, 2012 © AP Photo/Sergey Ponomarev/Press Association Images.

Ritual burial © Wolfgang Kaehler/Corbis Images.

Tree stump in Rathkeale, Ireland © PA/Press Association Images.

Jonestown mass suicide and killings, Guyana, 1978 © Sipa Press/Rex.

Atheist bus poster campaign © Rex/Glenn Copus/Evening Standard.

Depiction of Quetzalcoatl on temple at Teotihuacan, Mexico © Shutterstock.com

Sunday Assembly meeting, London © Rex/Nick Cunard.

Acknowledgments

I wish to thank Kristen Tate and Genevieve Shanahan for their helpful comments on various versions of the manuscript. Thanks also to Hilary Marsden for excellent copy-editing, and to George Miller for commissioning the book.

Index

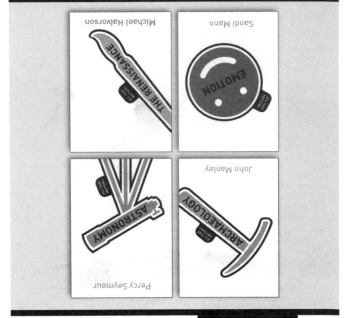

**Get to the heart of the most
talked about topics of our time**

www.allthatmatters.com

ALL THAT
MATTERS